Tips for Using This Book

I0468144

1. We have printed the pictures on one side of the page only to avoid pencil impression on next page and to protect each individual picture. A sheet of loose rough paper under the page you are working on will offer additional protection to the pages underneath.

2. Start with any page that grabs your interest- who says you need to start from the beginning?

3. Be FREE and color how you desire. There is no thumb rule. There is no "WRONG" way.

4. For the Stress-Relieving coloring experience, Reduce noise and other distractions while coloring. Coloring with Focus and Intention is calming and nurturing for your spirit

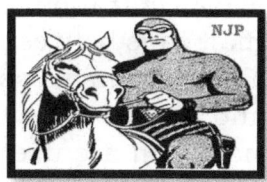

Digital Comics World
By: Satyanveshi
Copyright © 2016

All rights reserved. May not be replicated or reprinted without written permission from the publisher.

Introduction

Mandala is a Sanskrit word for circle. It has a spiritual significance, and is a famous symbol for Buddhists and Hindus, which represent Universe. The primary Mandala design depicts a square with four gates. All the gates look like the alphabet T. The design also has a circle in the middle. Mandalas are known to portray radial balance.

The Sanskrit term is known to be mentioned in Rig Veda, which is a section of its work. It also takes a major part in philosophy and religion, especially for Buddhists. There are many spiritual traditions which include Mandala for focusing on attention and concentration. Mandala coloring pages are a form of art, which emphasize on this note.

The mandala coloring pages are suitable for both old and young. Some of the designs are quite complicated, and they need quite a lot of skill and effort to be colored. Thus, they aren't advisable for children but are for adults instead. If you want to choose Mandala prints for your children, you should look for the ones which are a little less complicated and have simpler shapes.

The levels of detail in these shapes are very minute, for which advanced painters and adults would enjoy them more. You could come across areas which are difficult to be colored with crayons, thus you'd need some fine tipped coloring pencils or markers fill up those gaps.

Mandala is used in numerous religious traditions. The mandala coloring pages are primarily created to promote concentration in the painter's minds. While they try to fill up the small gaps between the bordered lines, they simultaneously have better focusing skills. These are a major gateway to meditation and trance-induction. Mandalas are surely generic forms of diagrams which are used for charts and geometry. These give you a basic idea of cosmos, both symbolically and metaphysically.

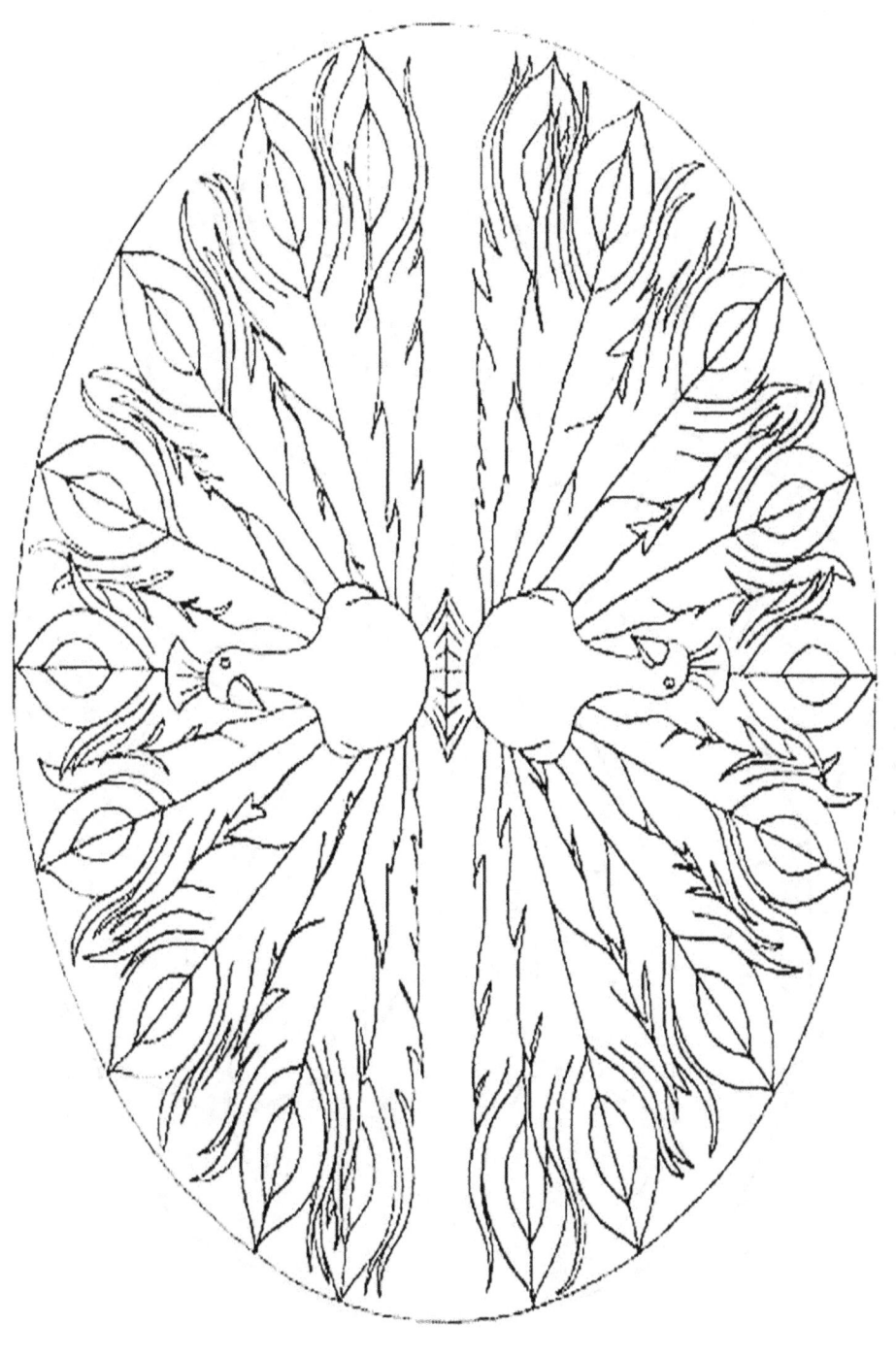

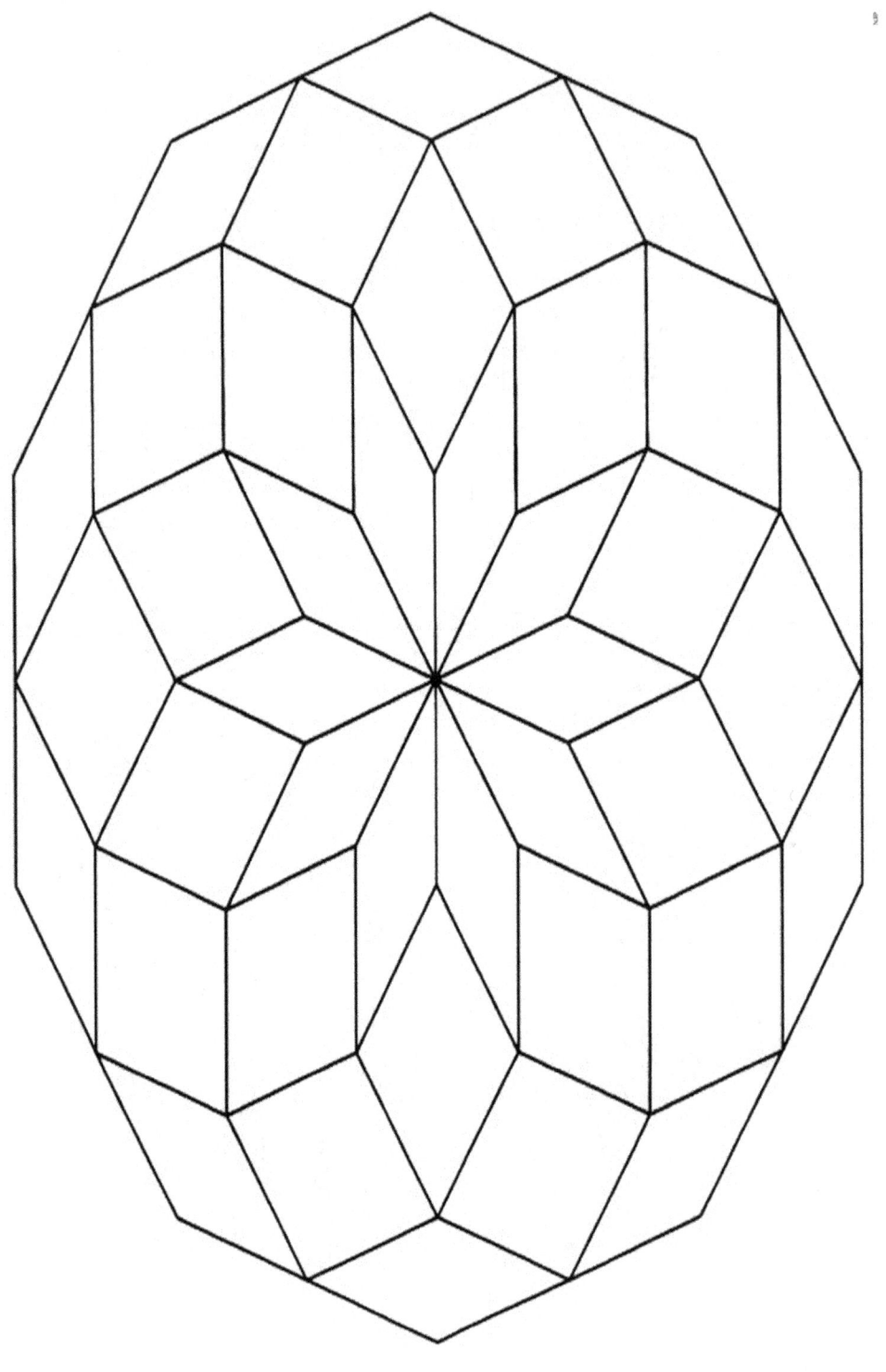

4

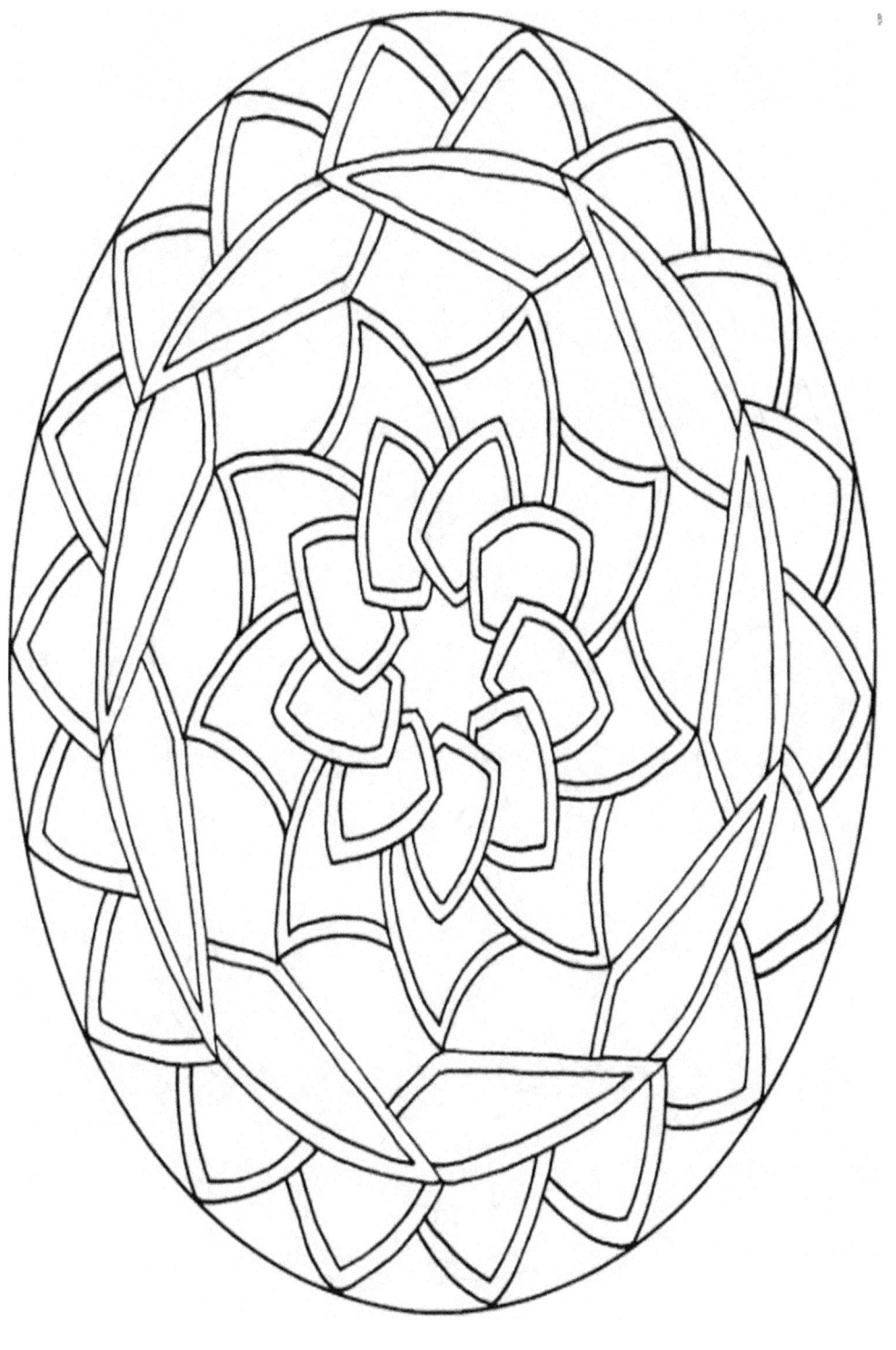

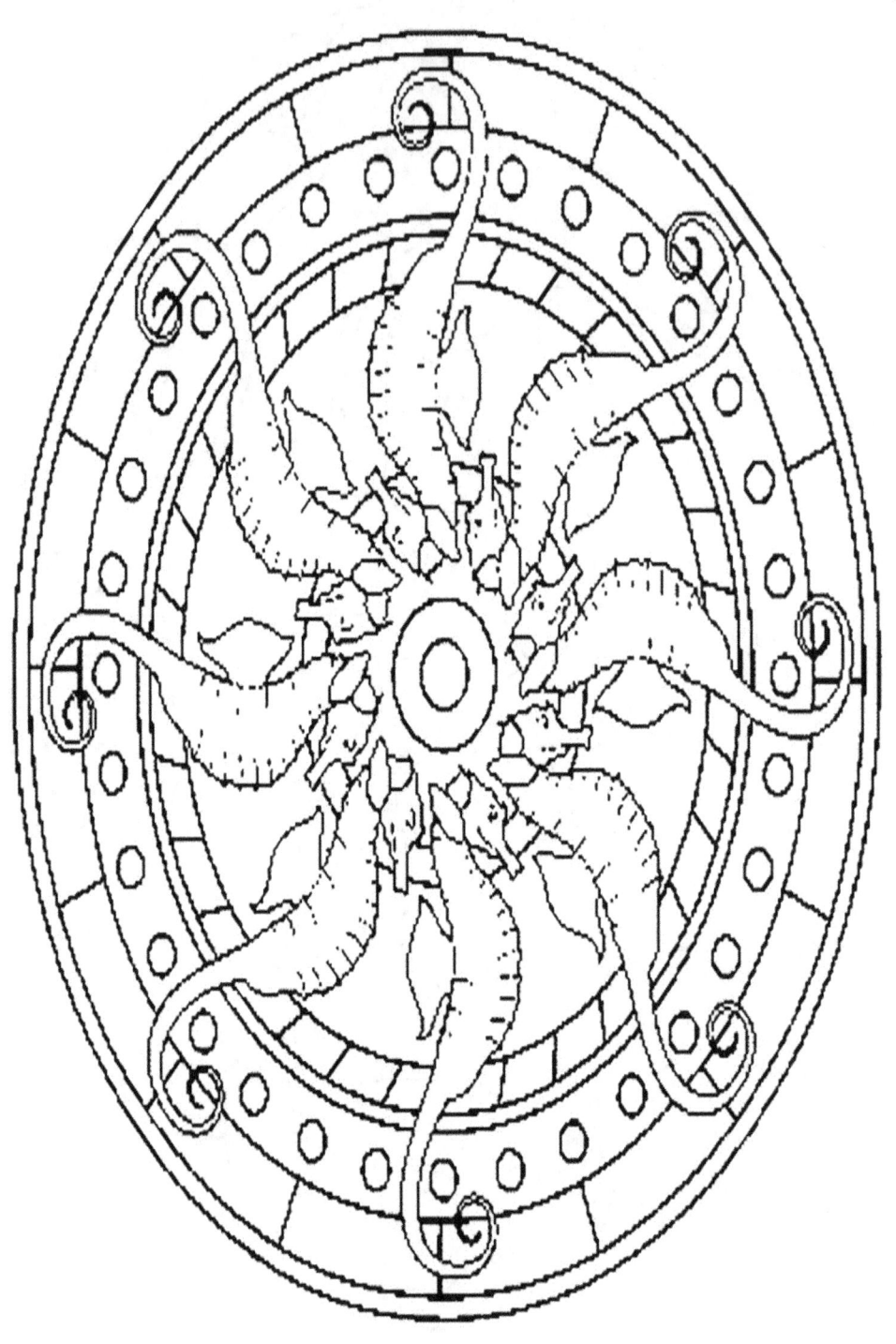

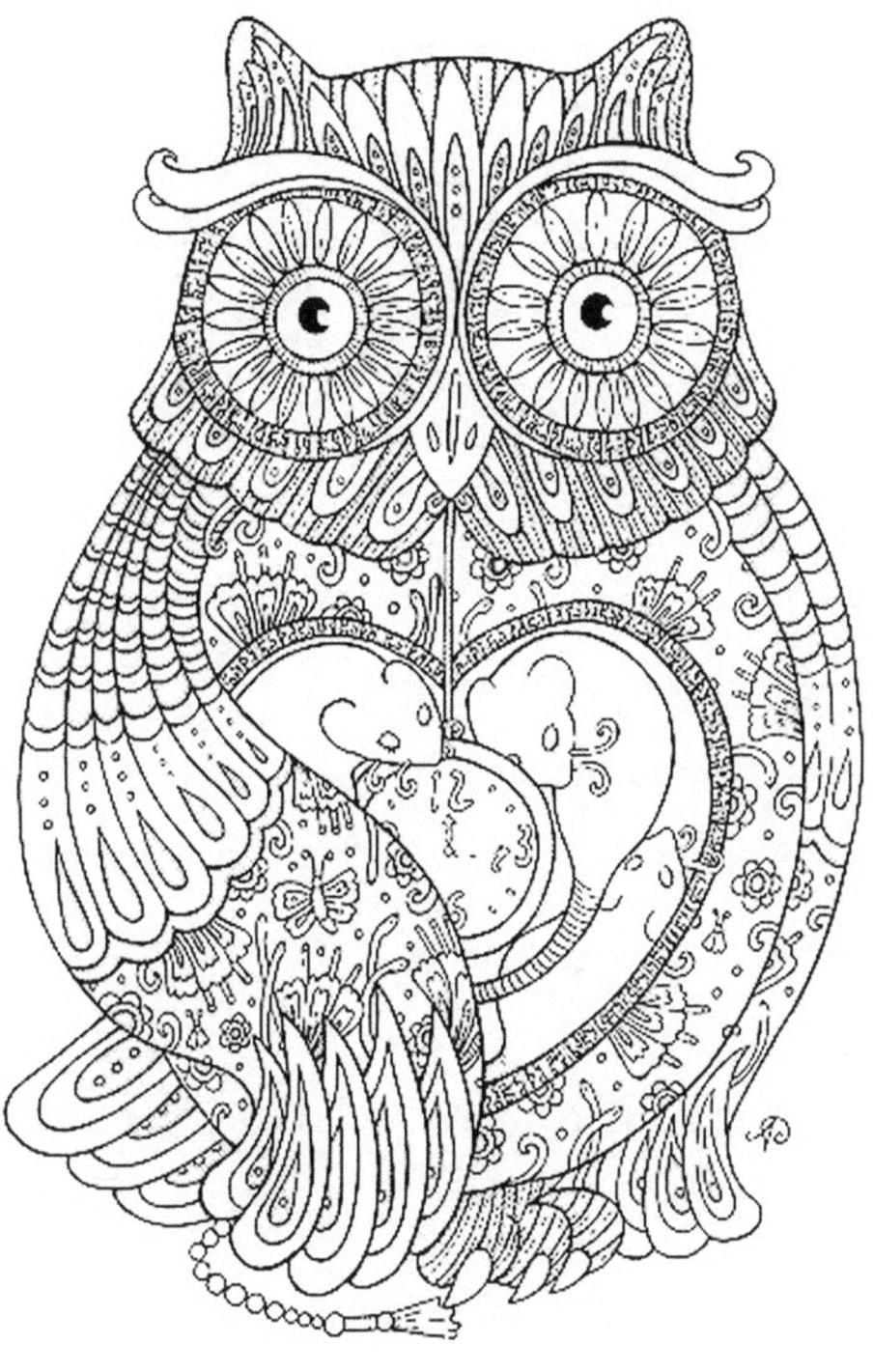

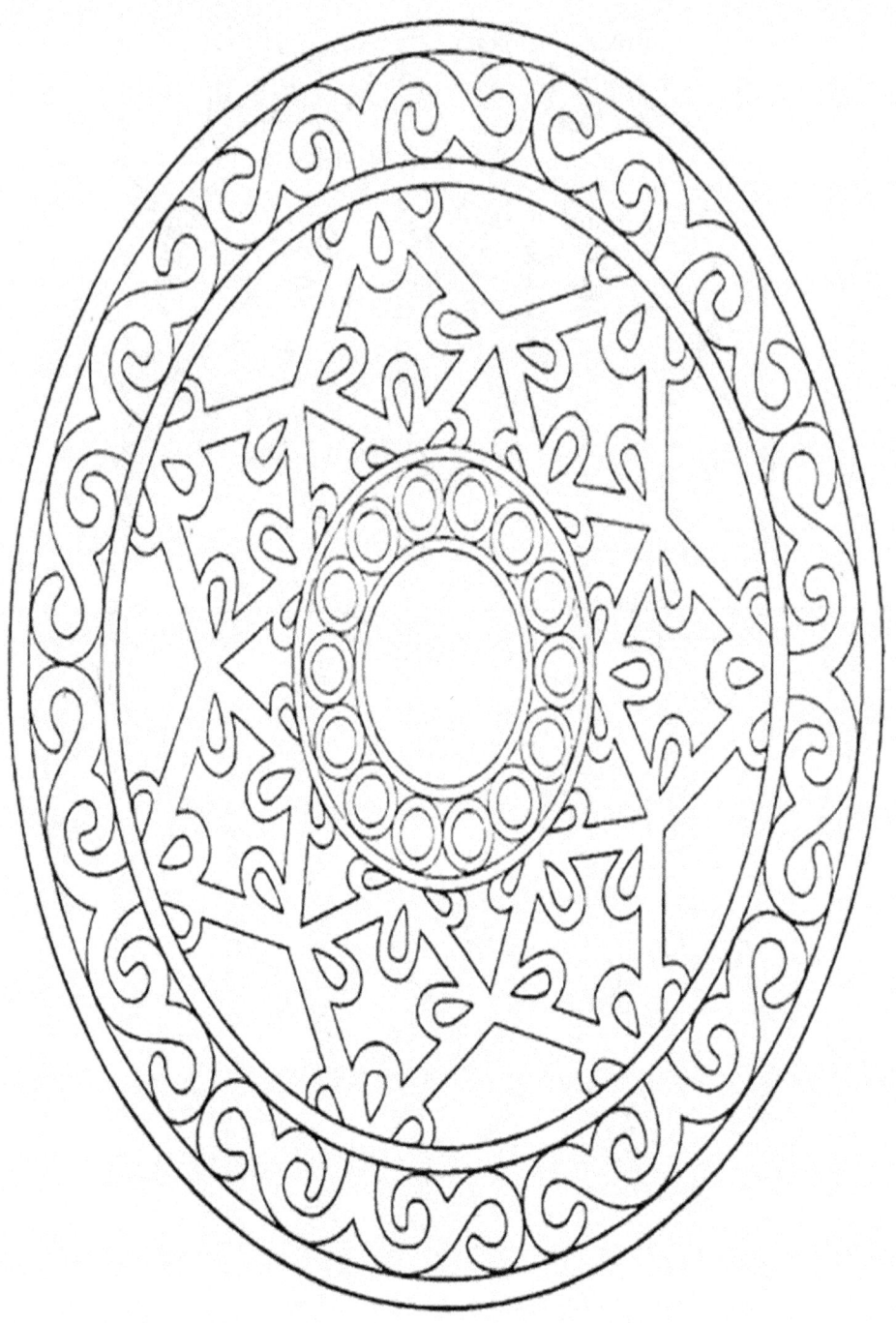

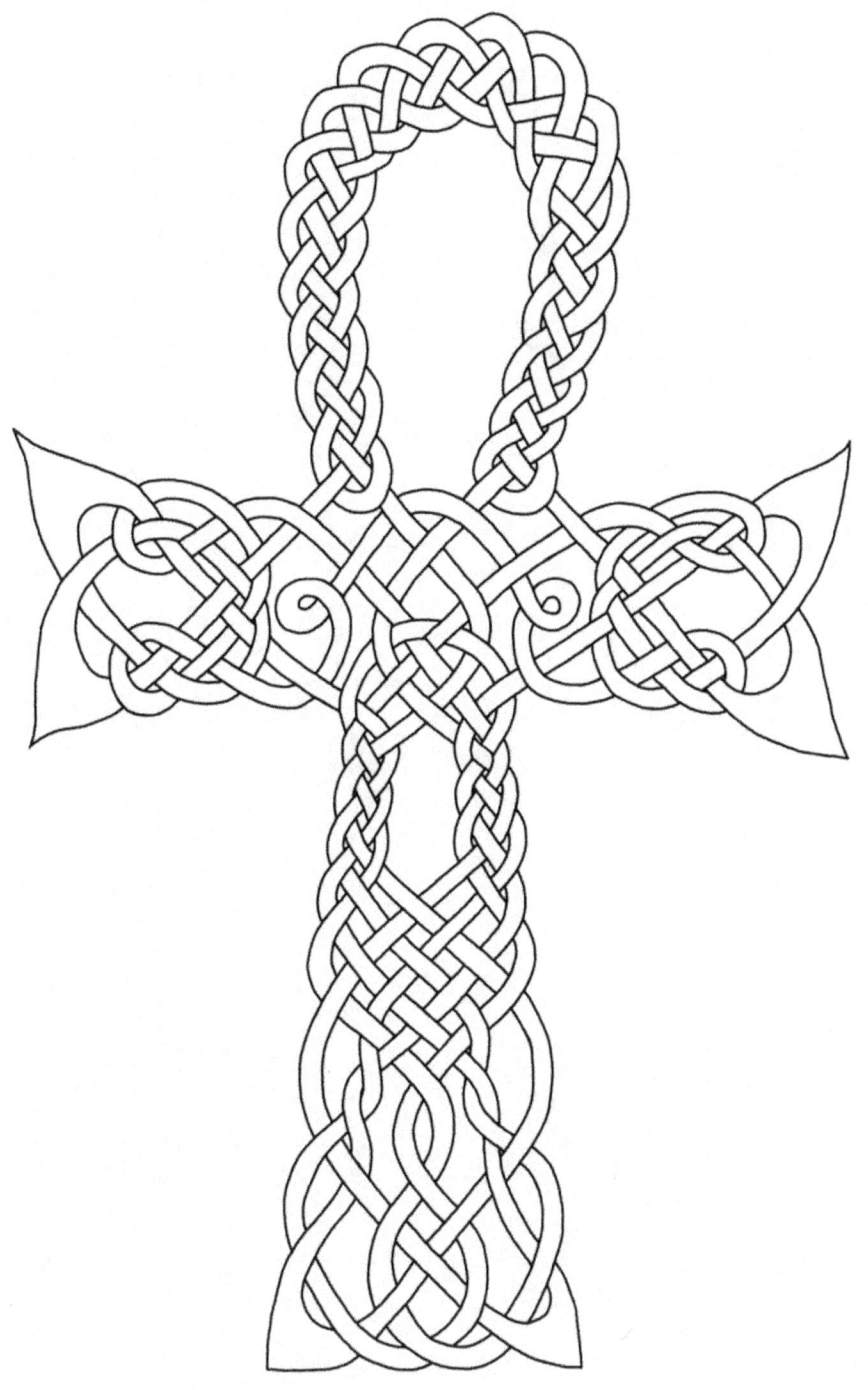

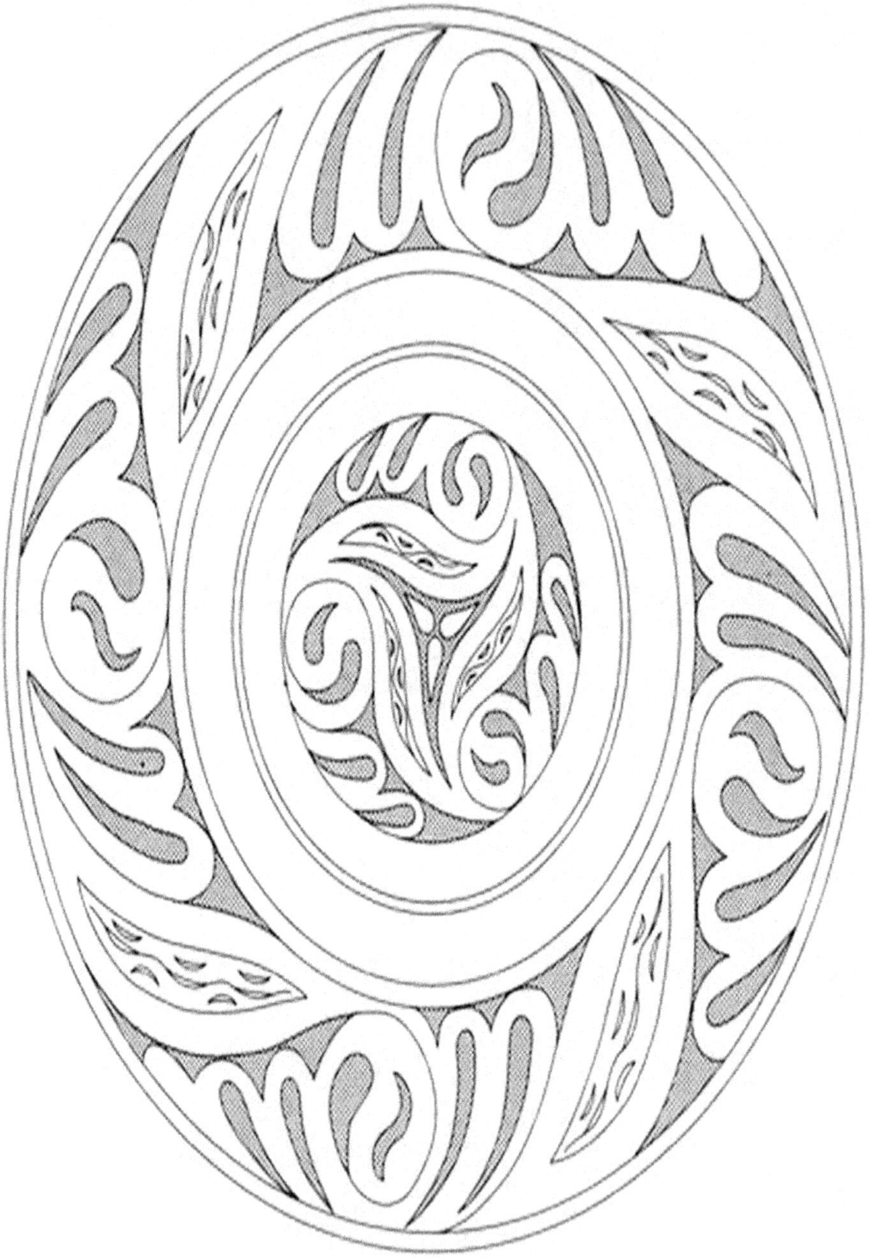

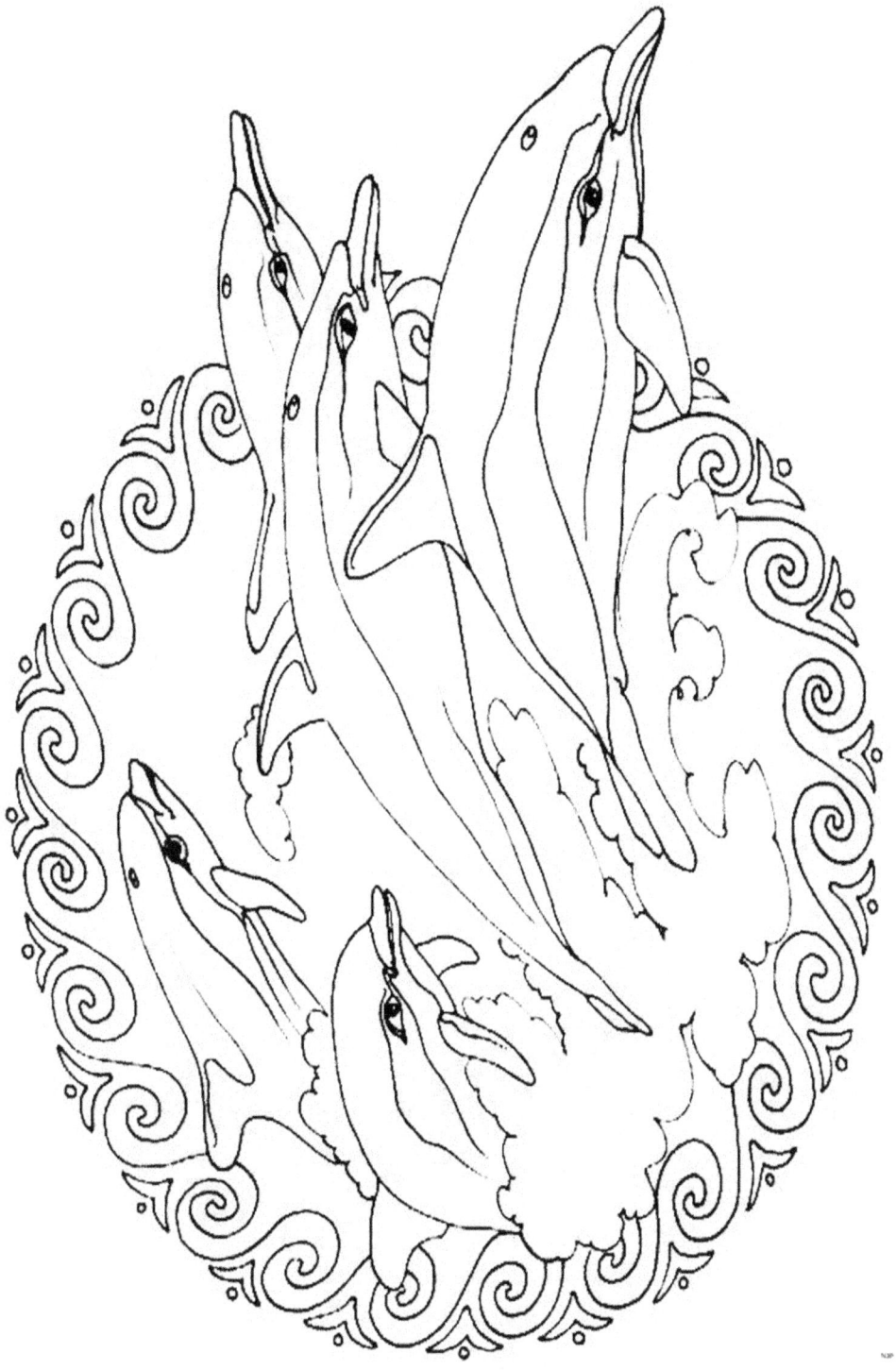

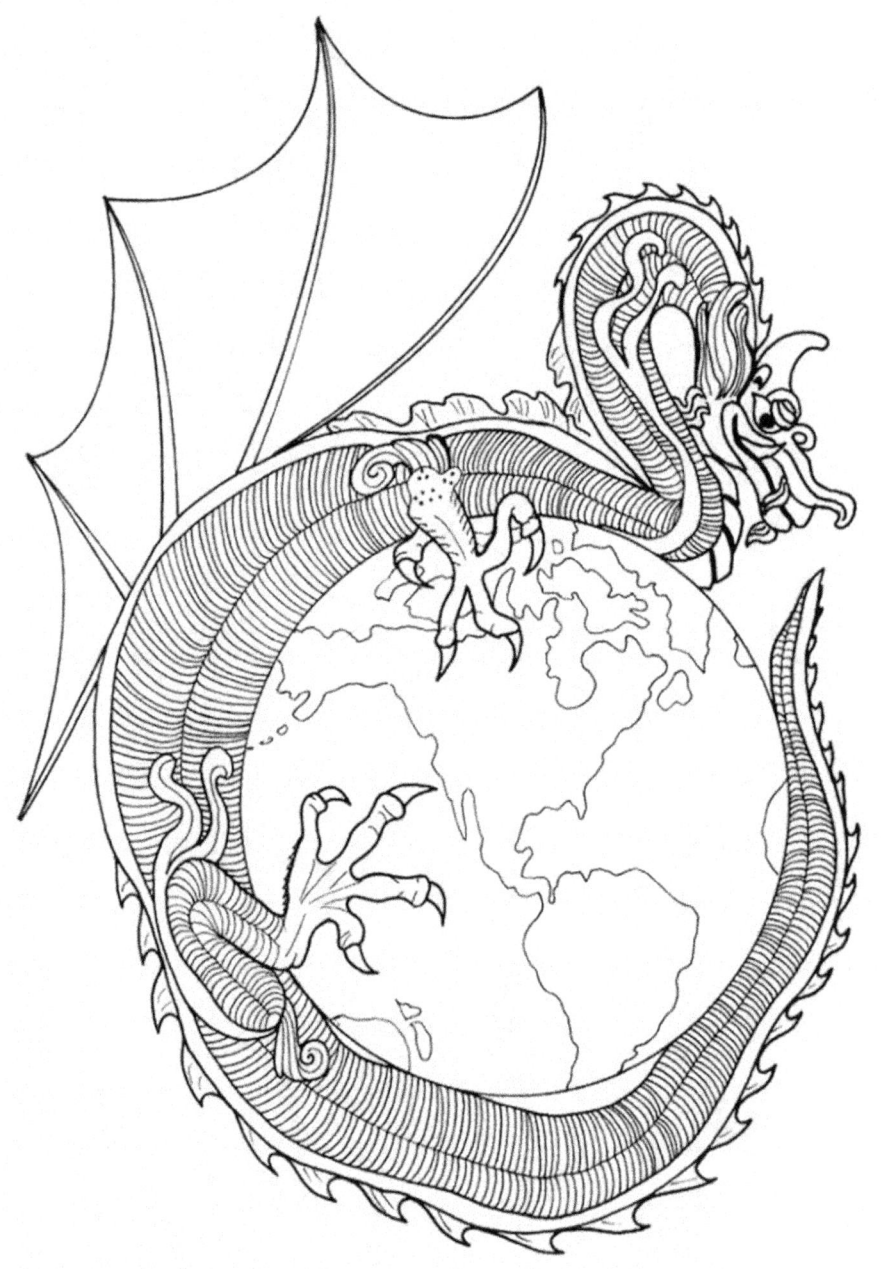

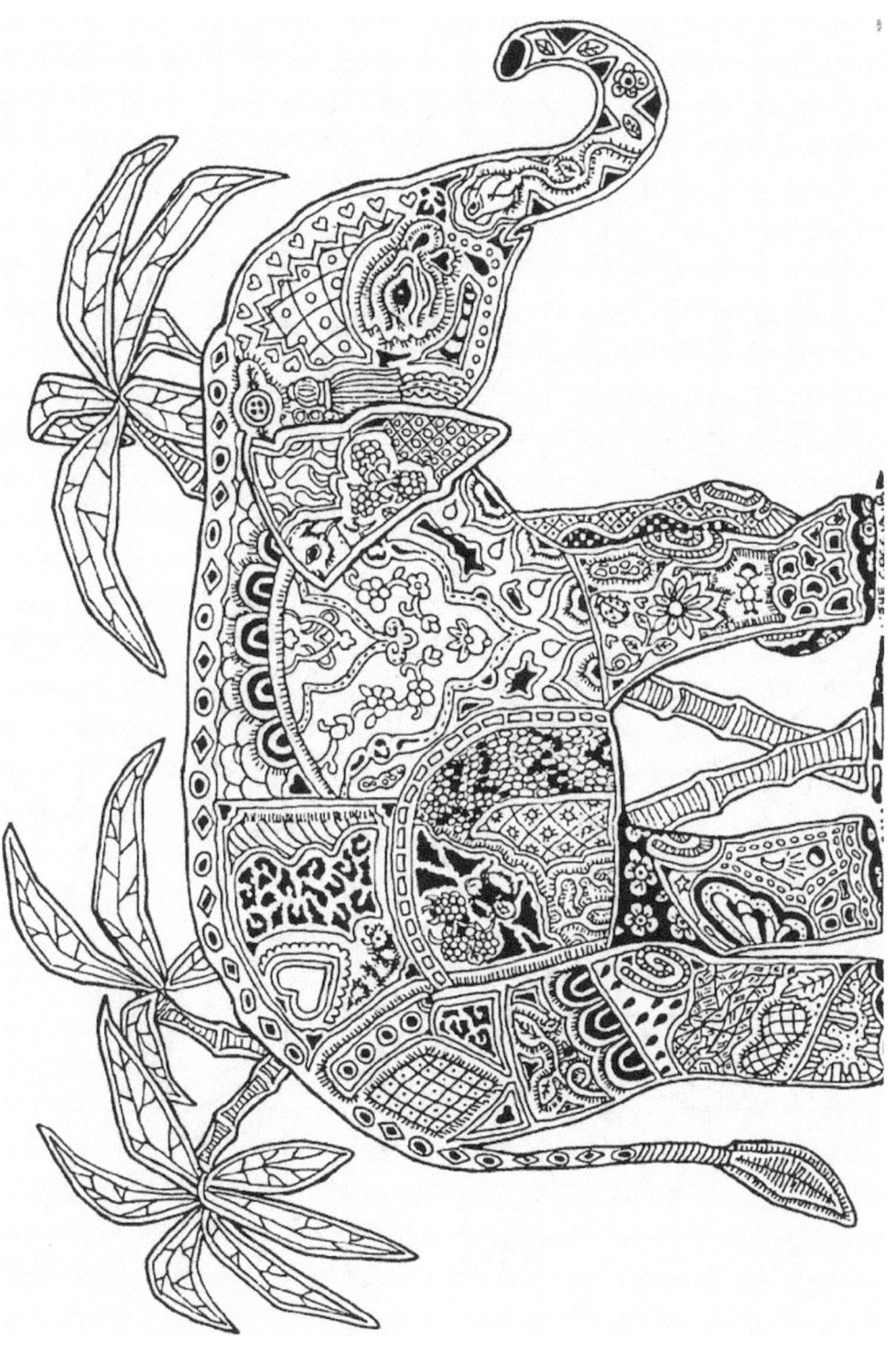

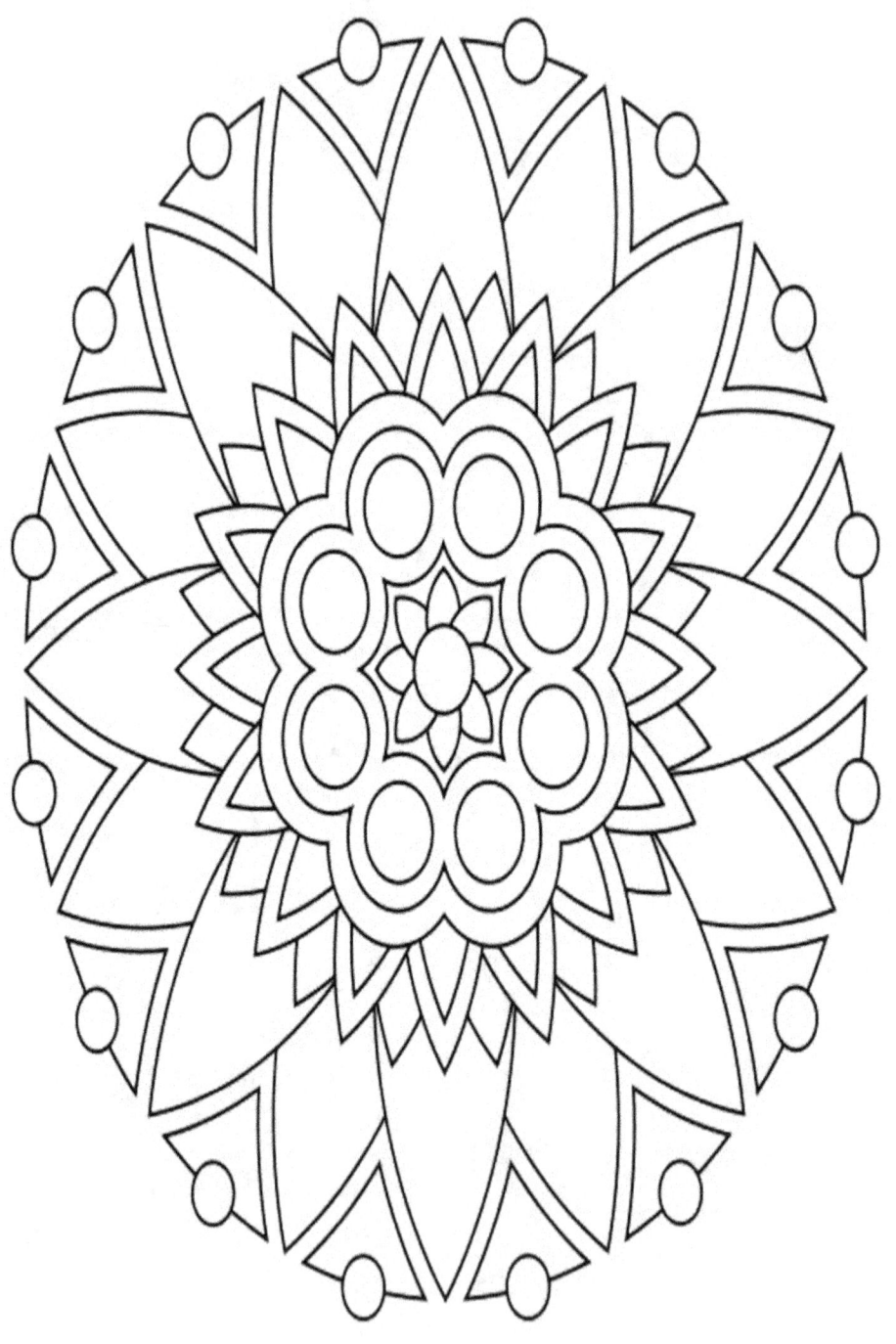

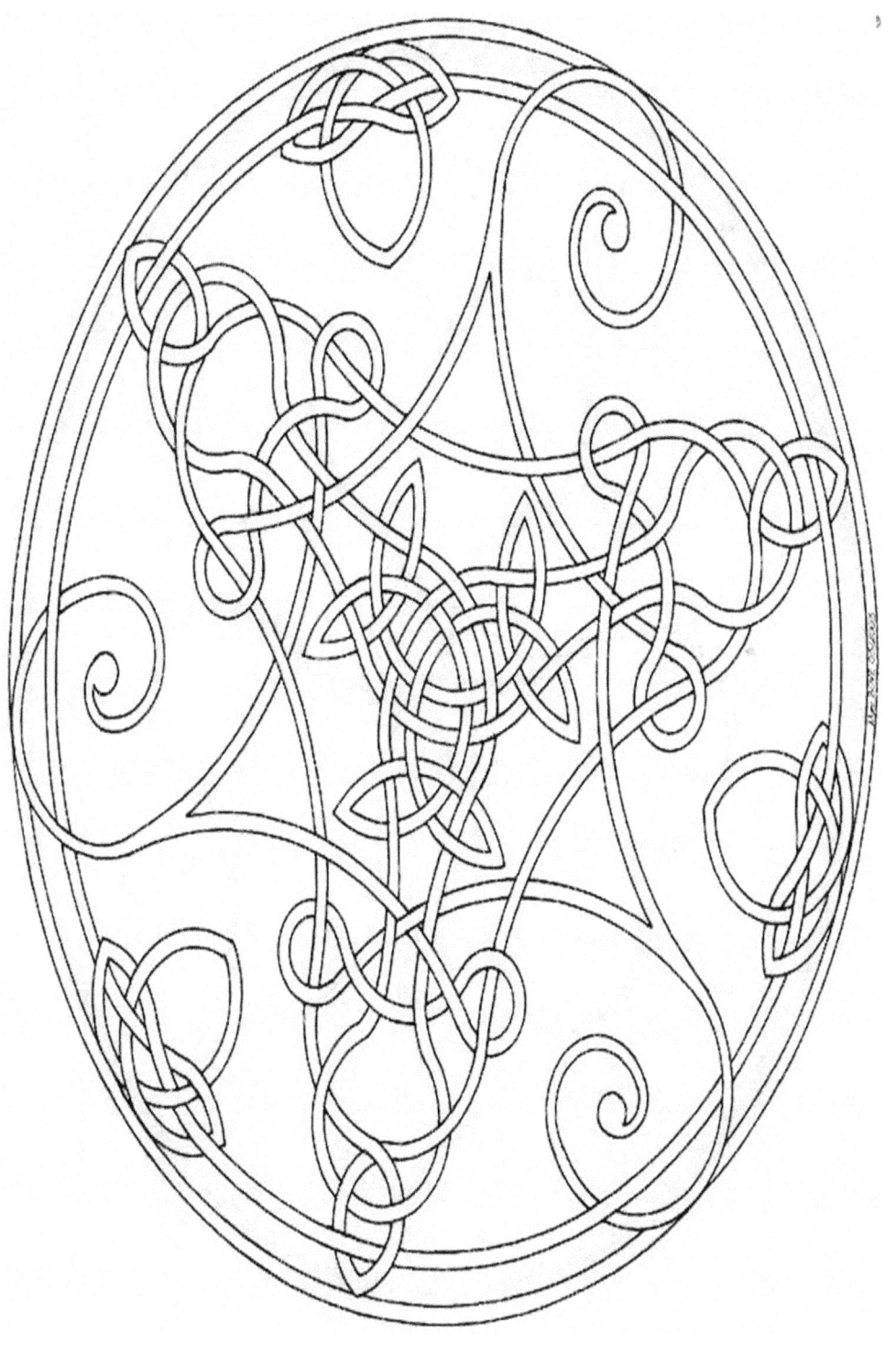

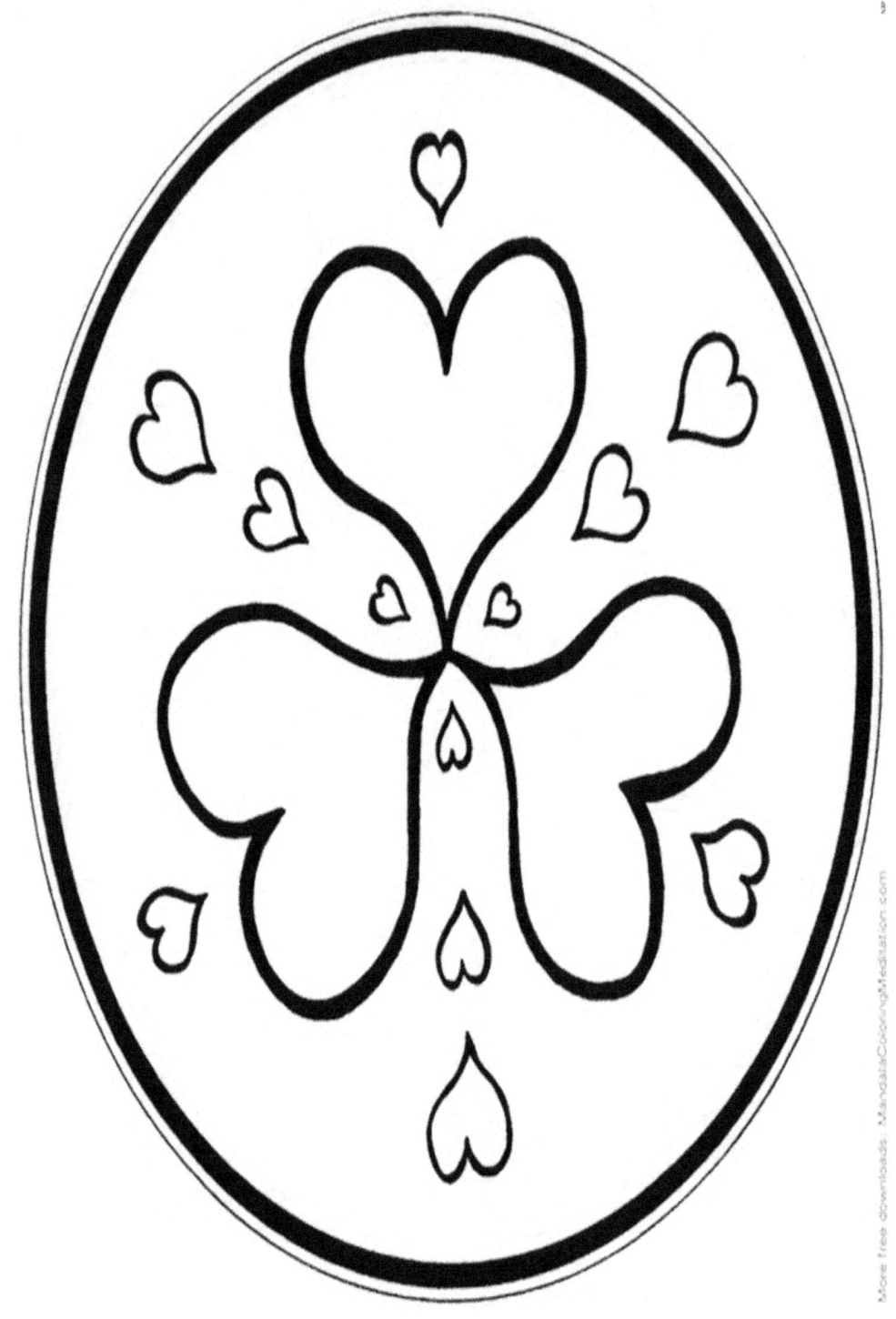

More free downloads: MandalaColoringMeditation.com

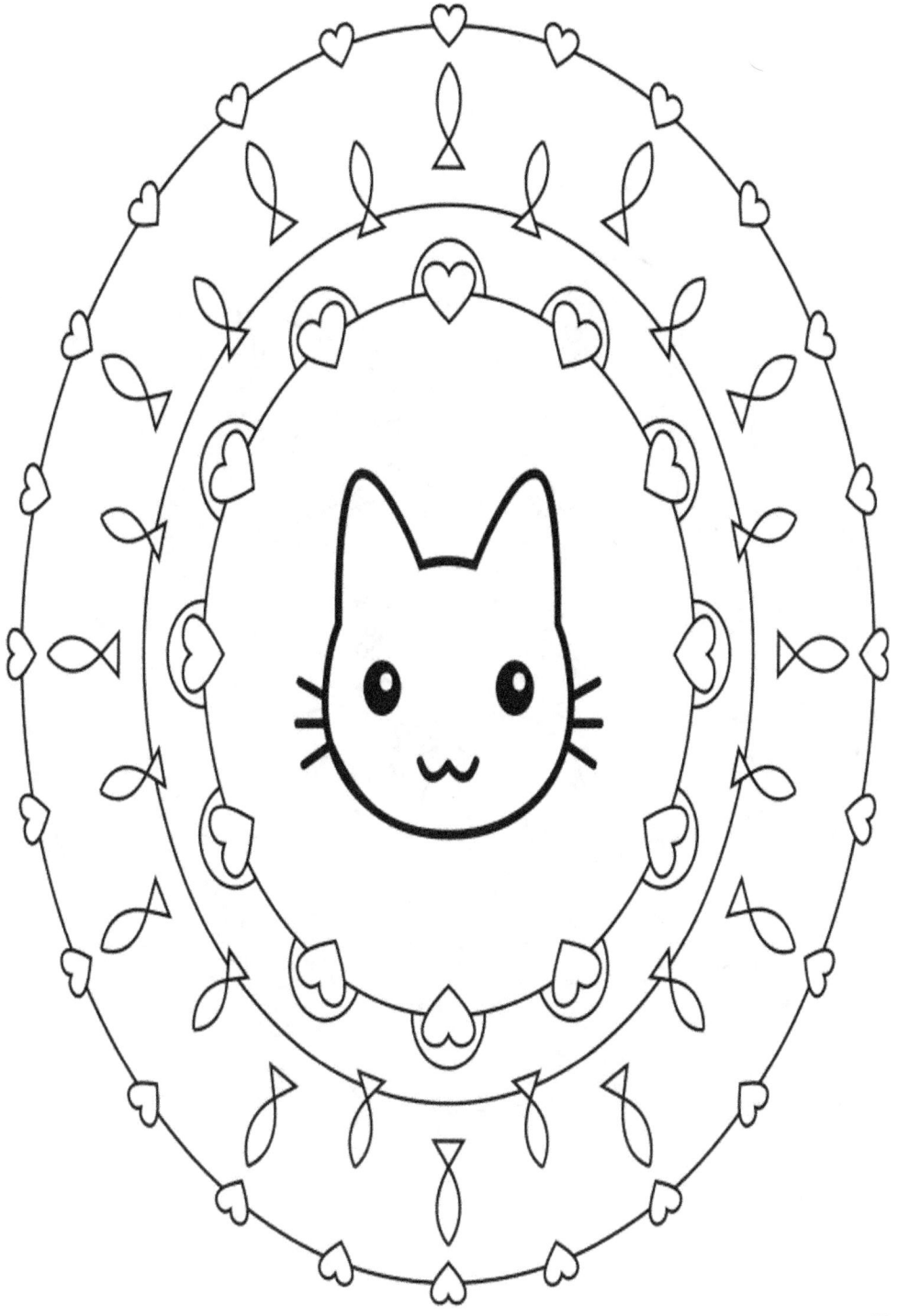

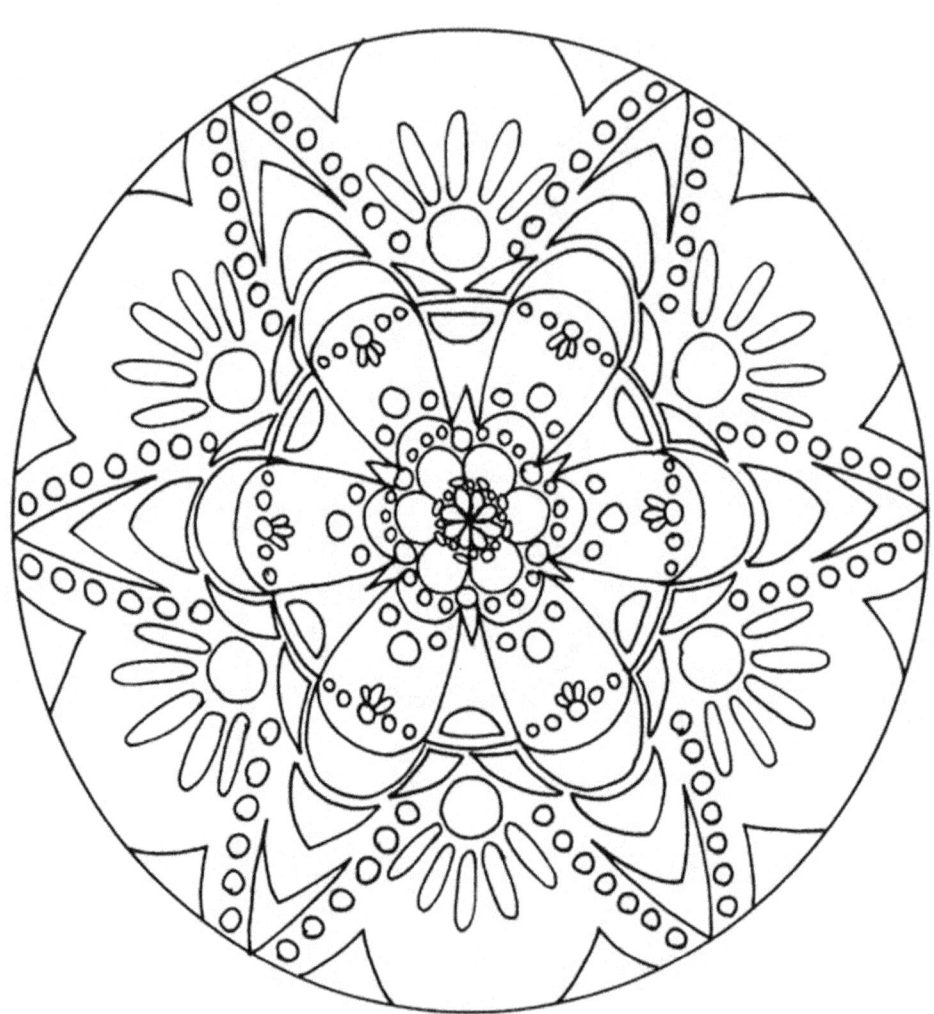

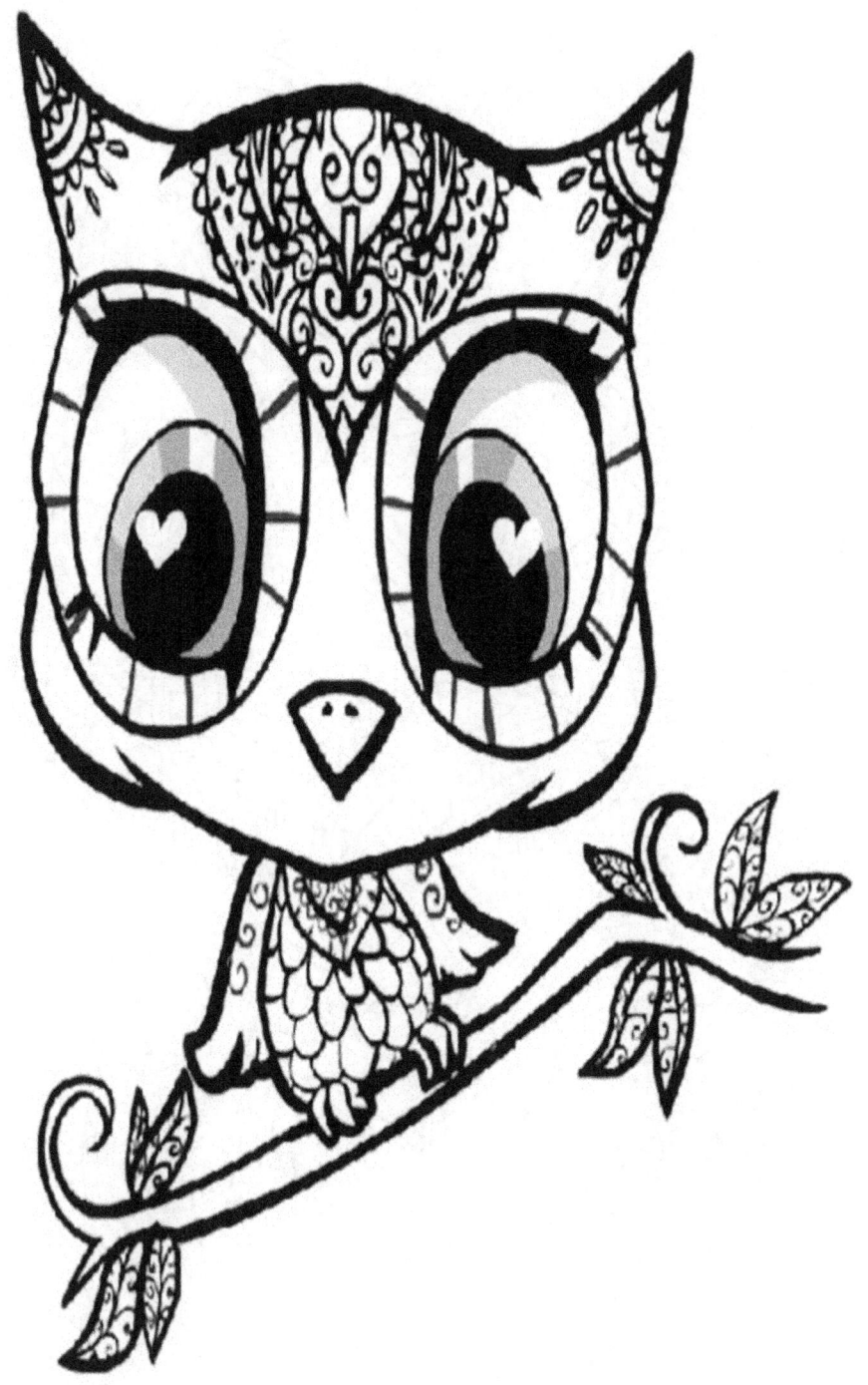

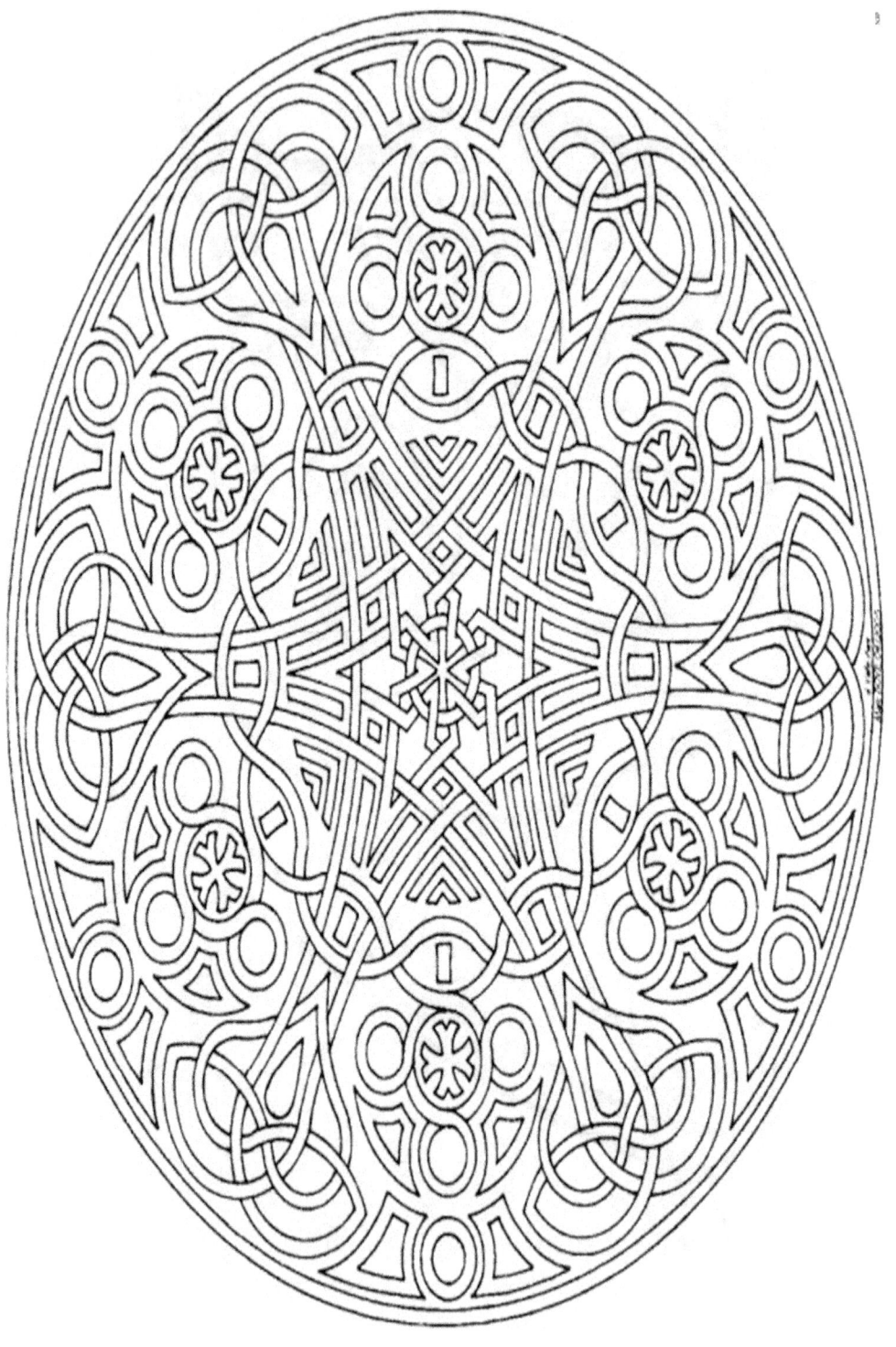

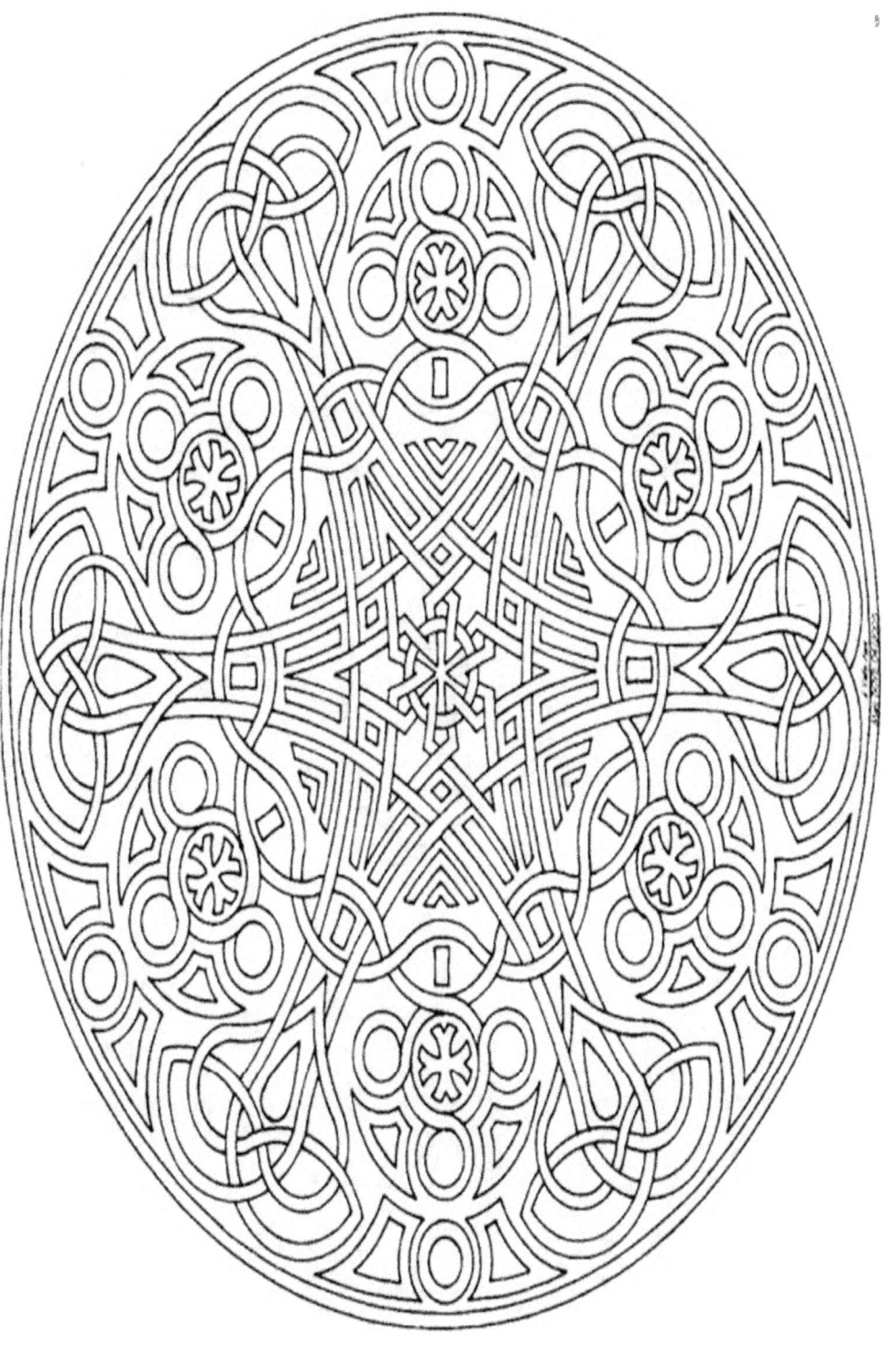

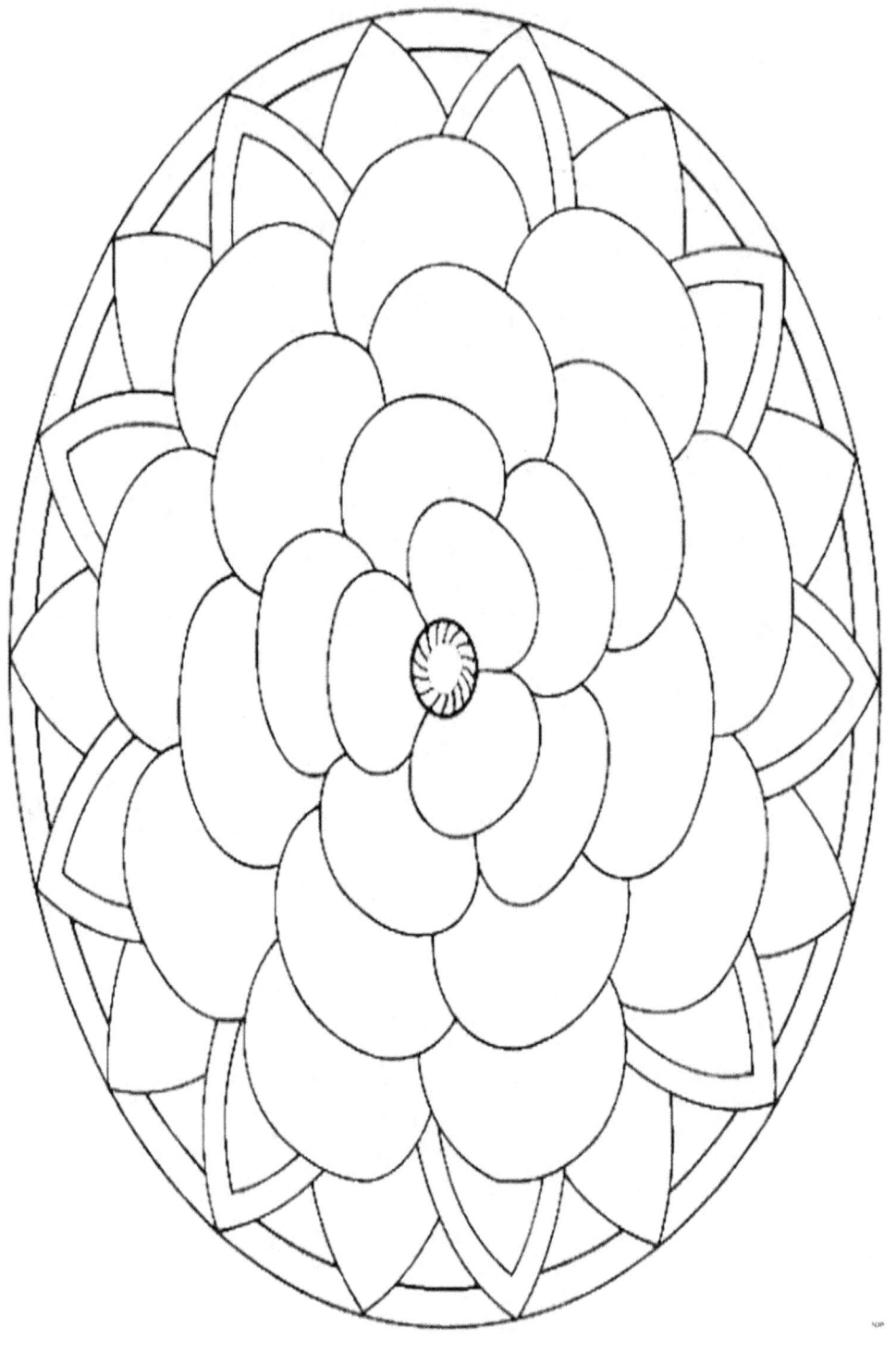

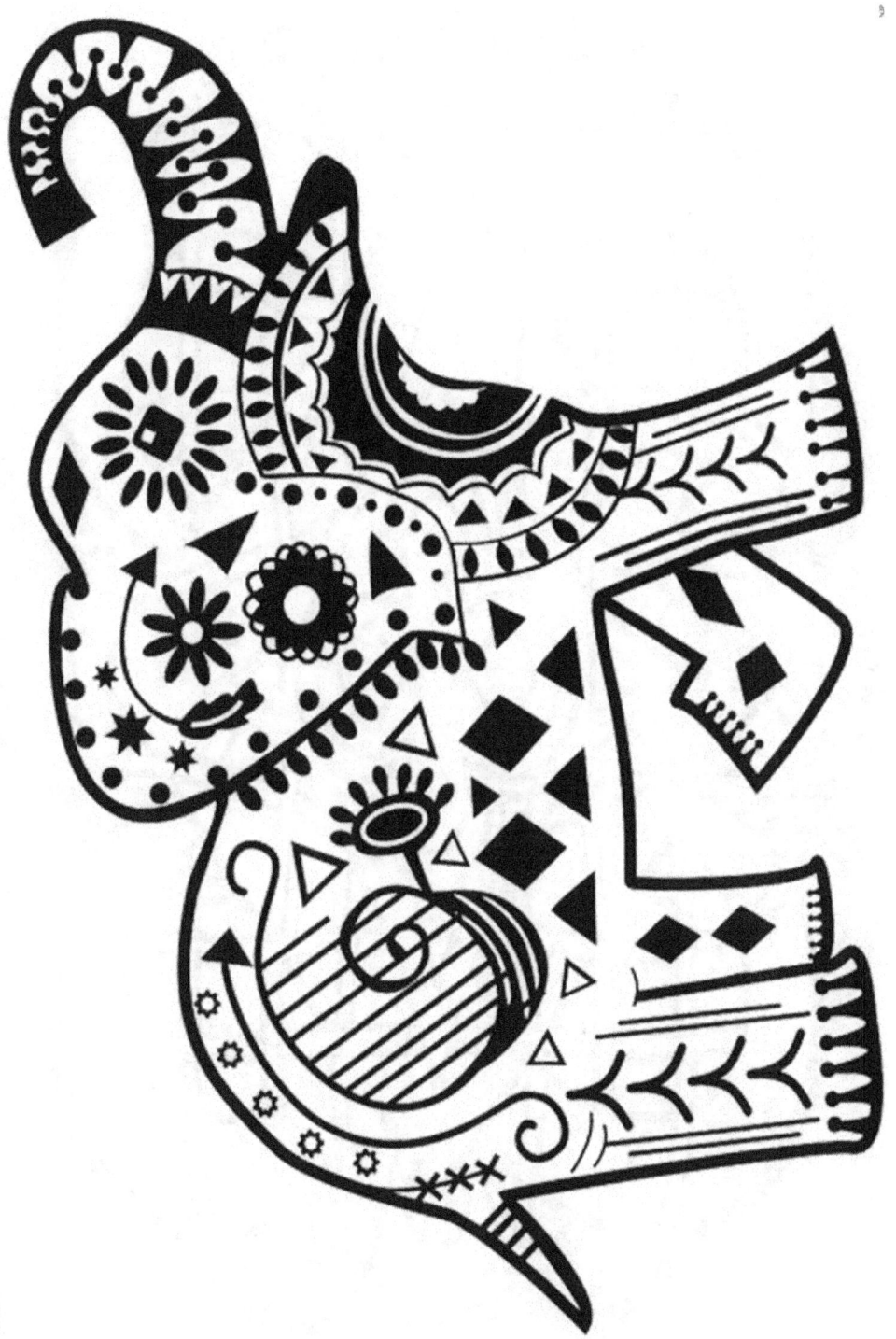

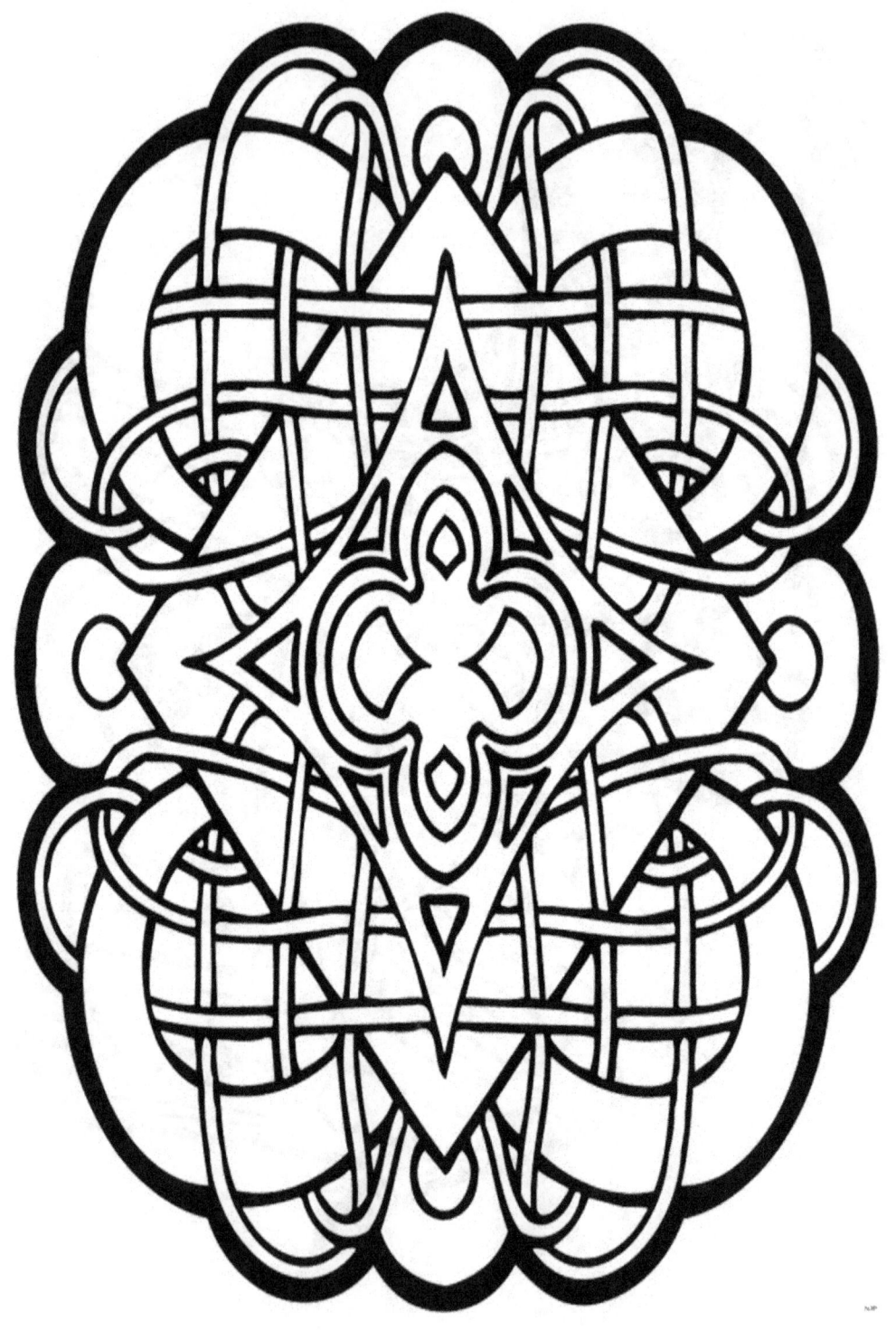

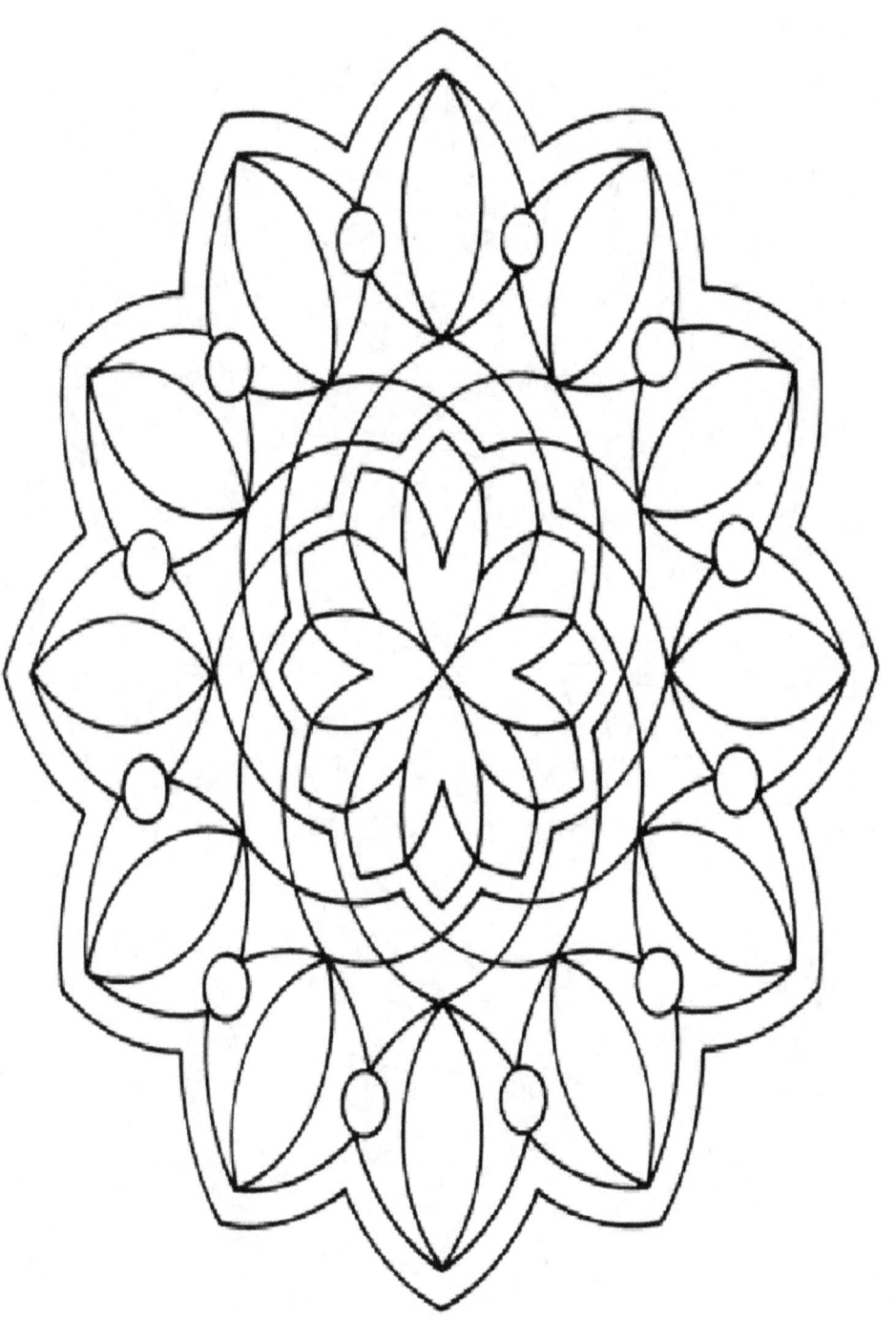

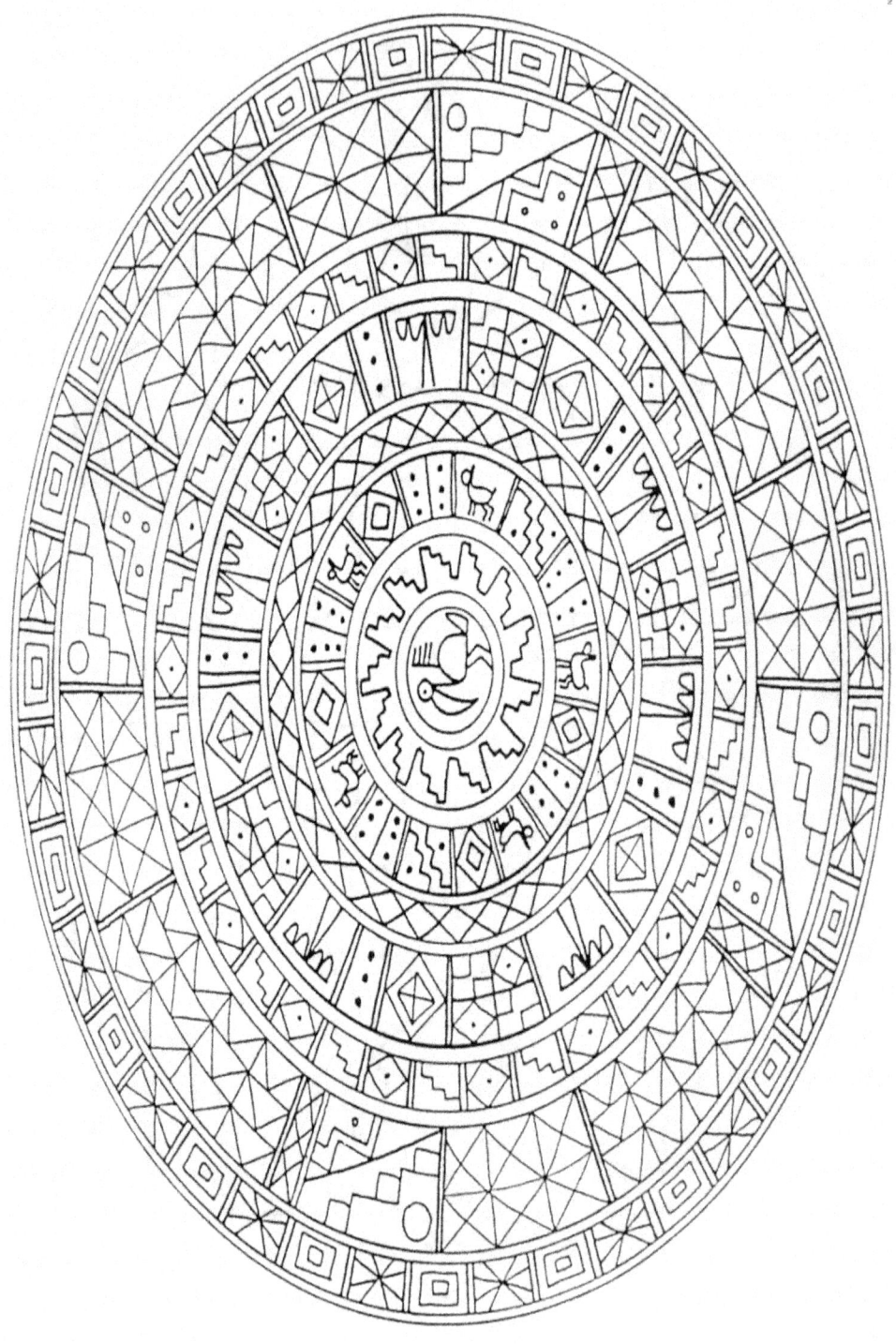

26

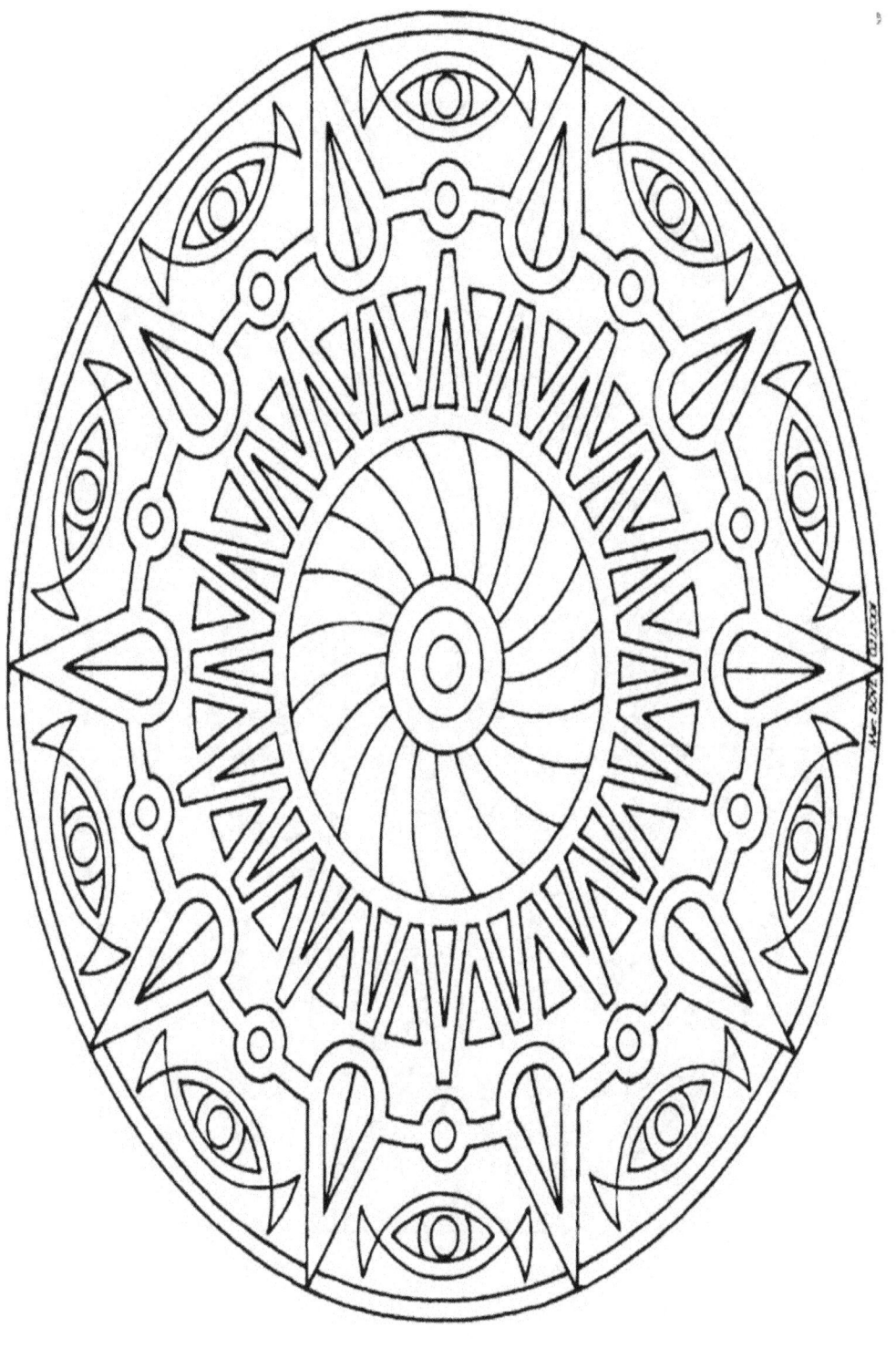

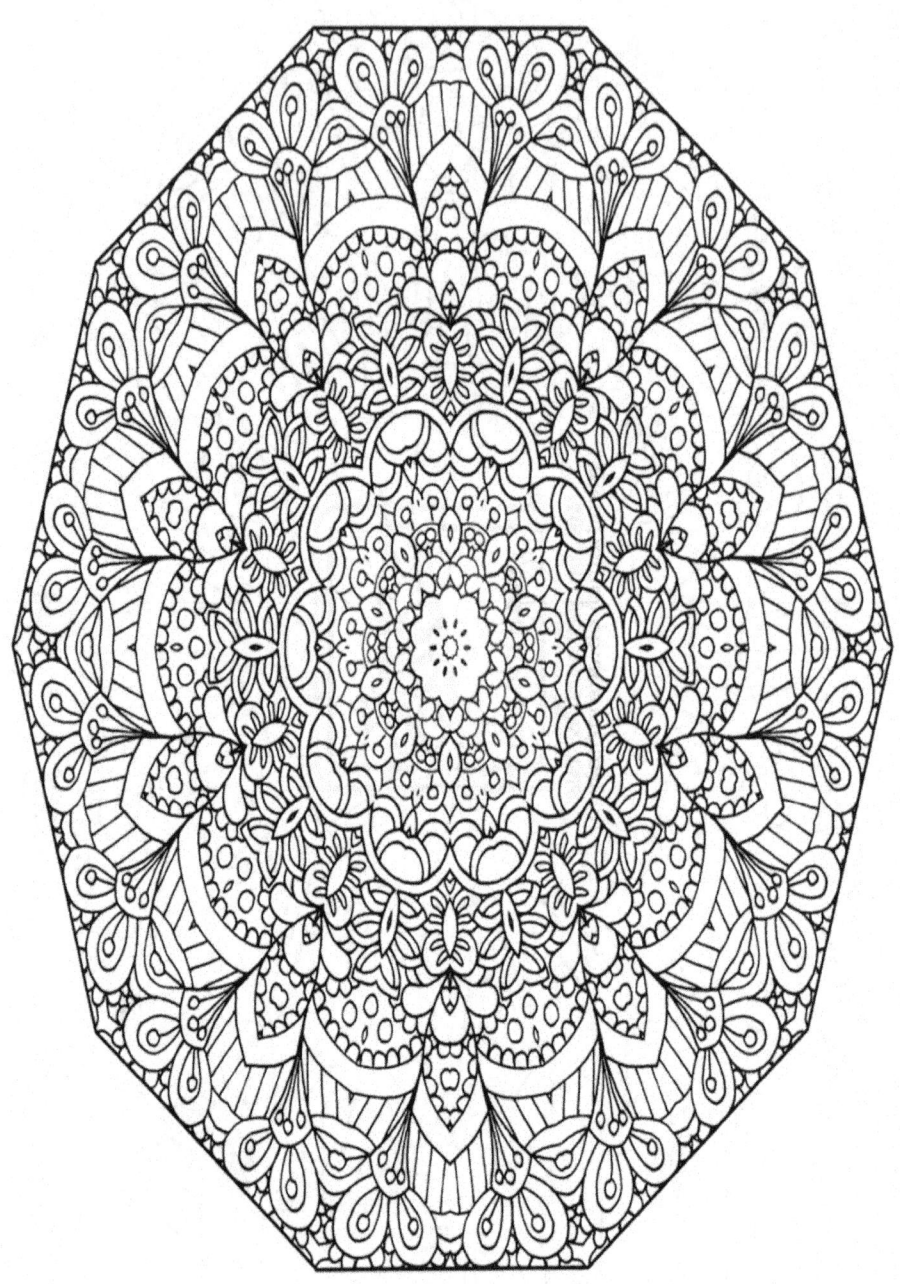

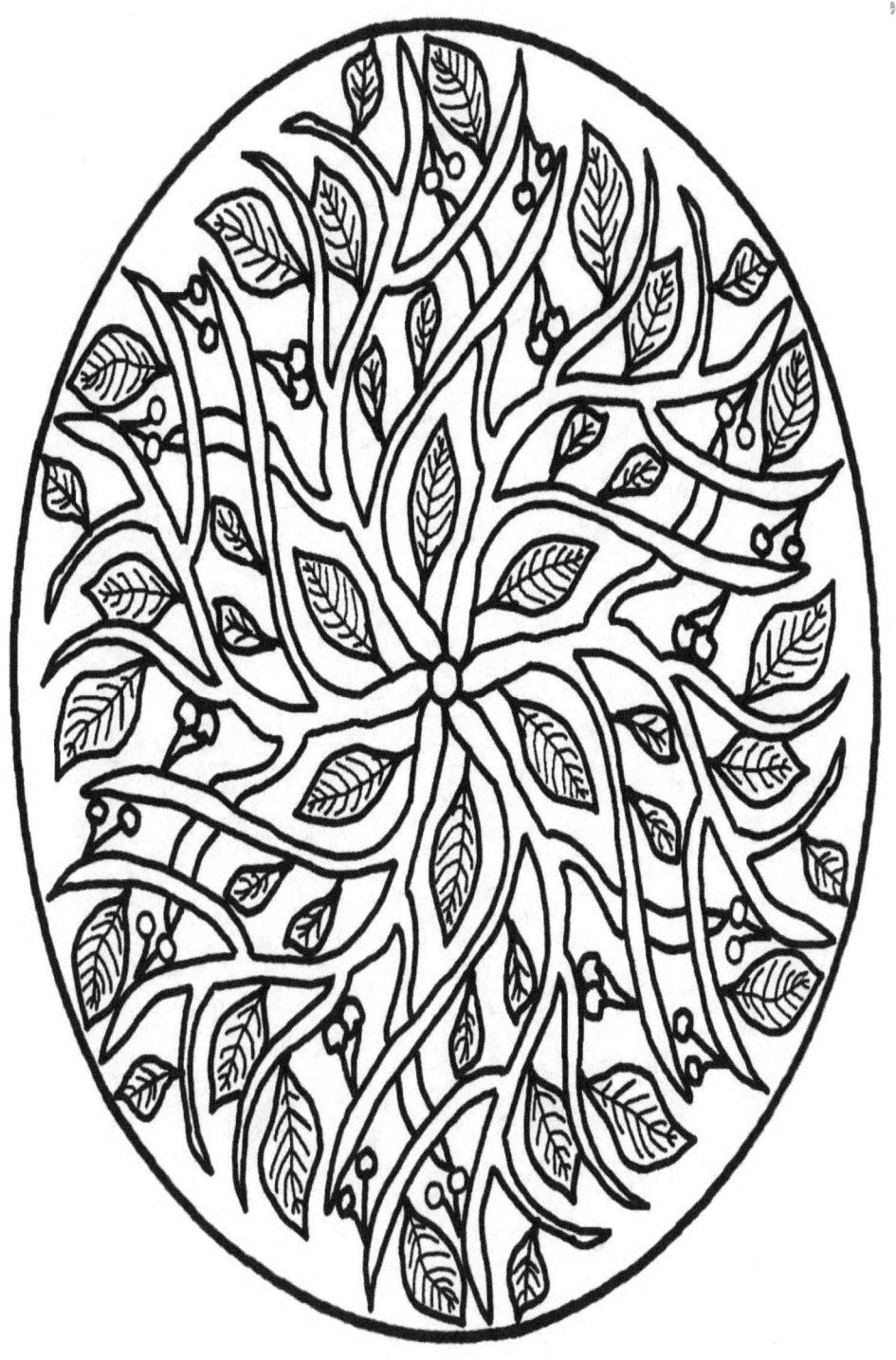

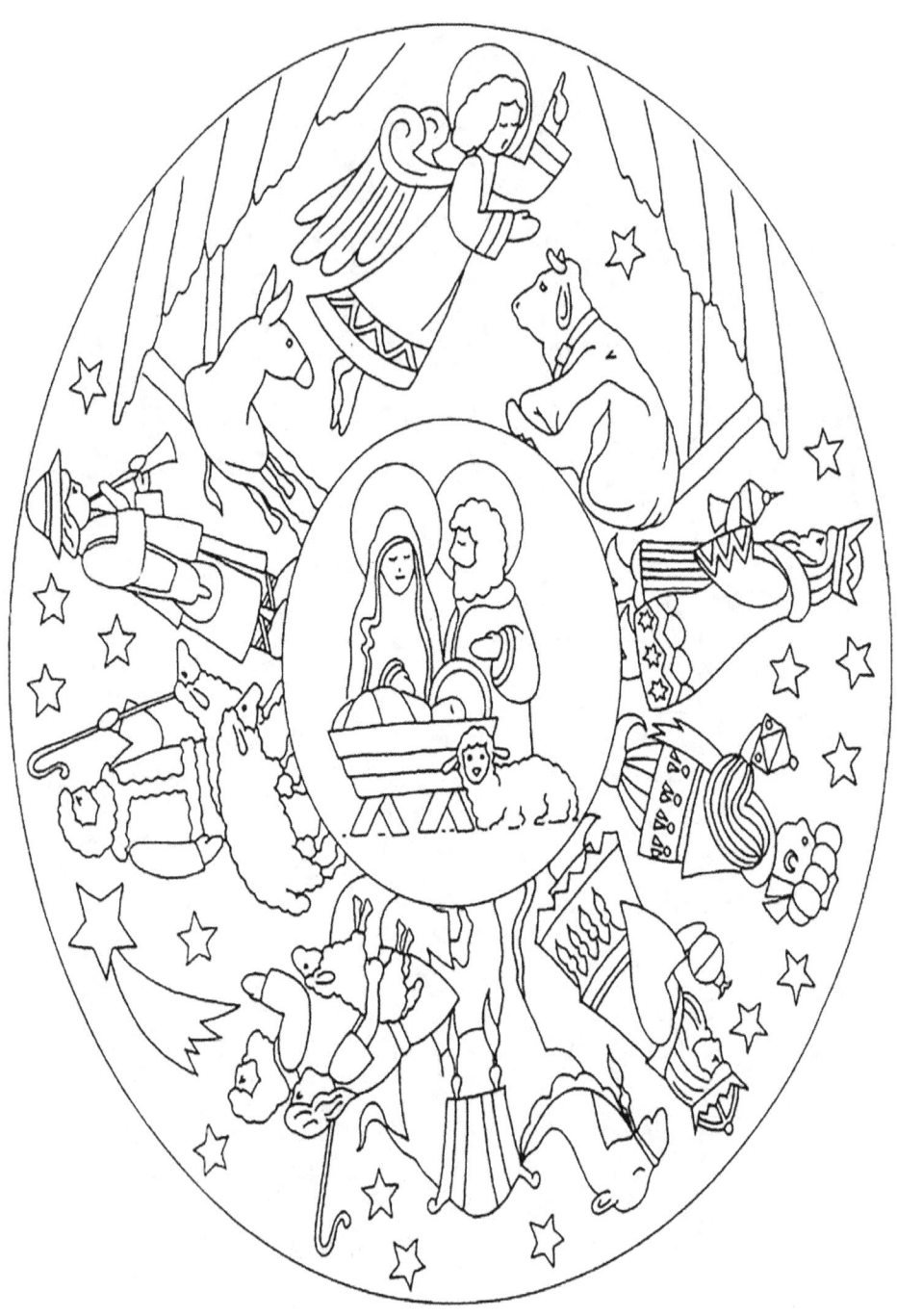

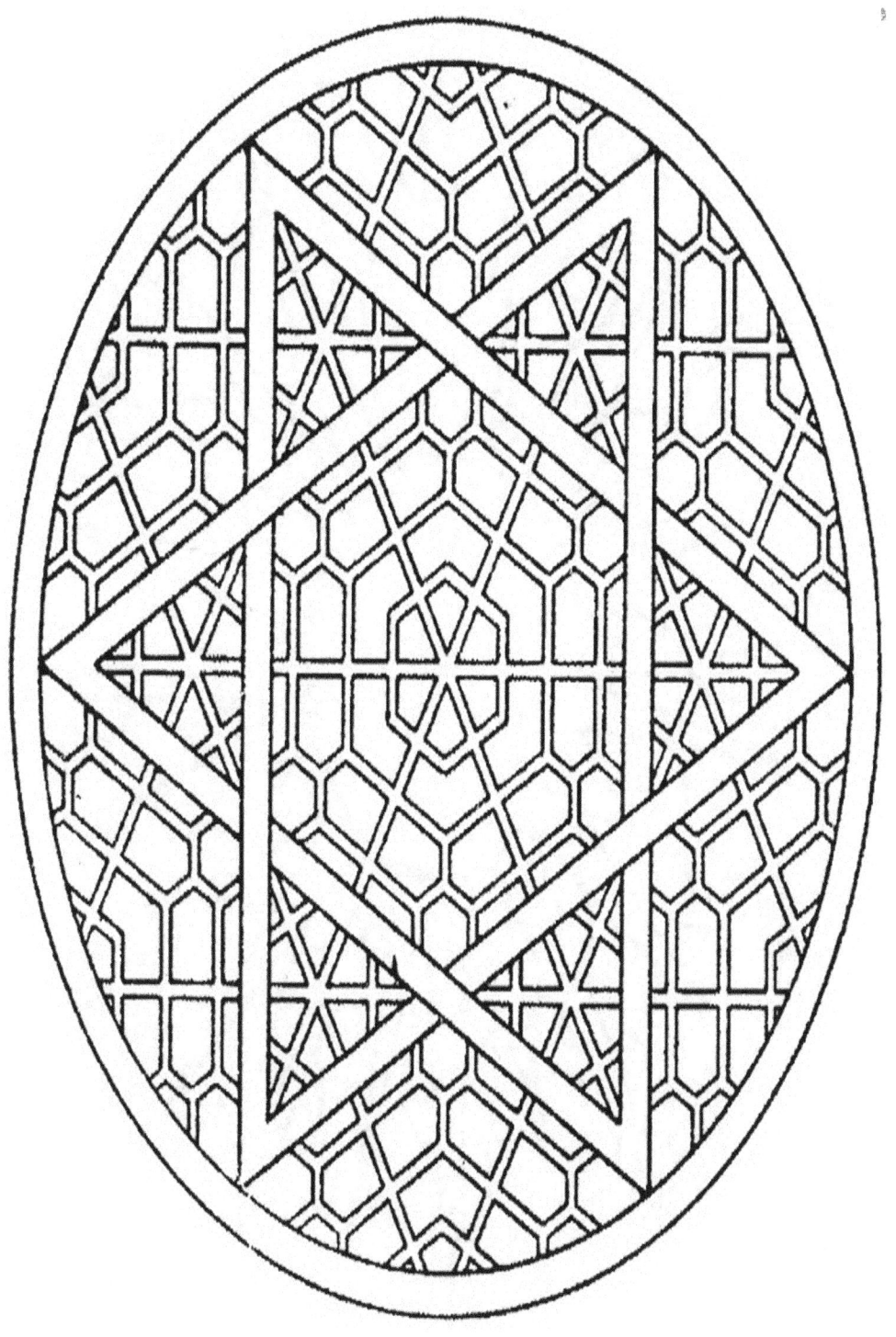

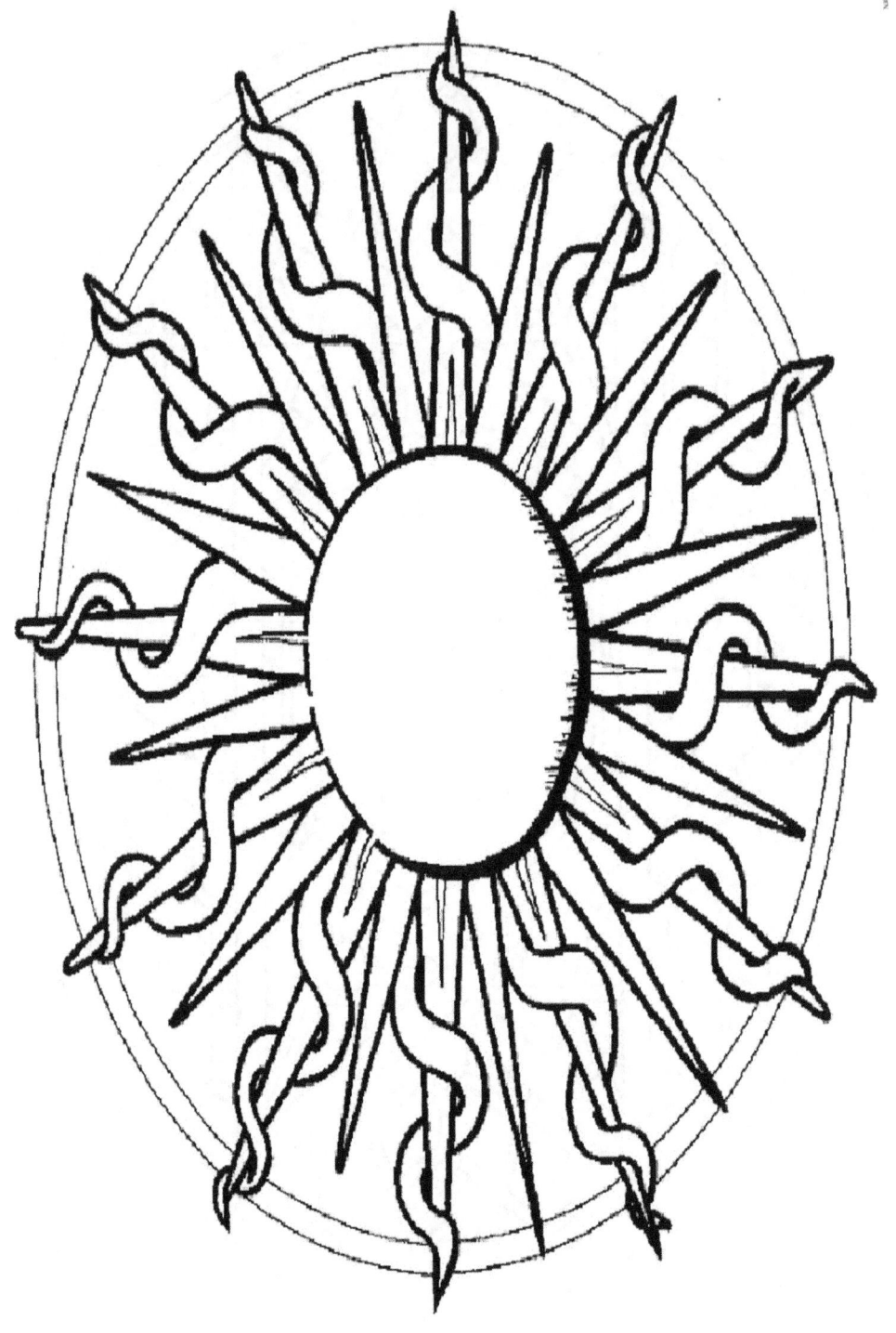

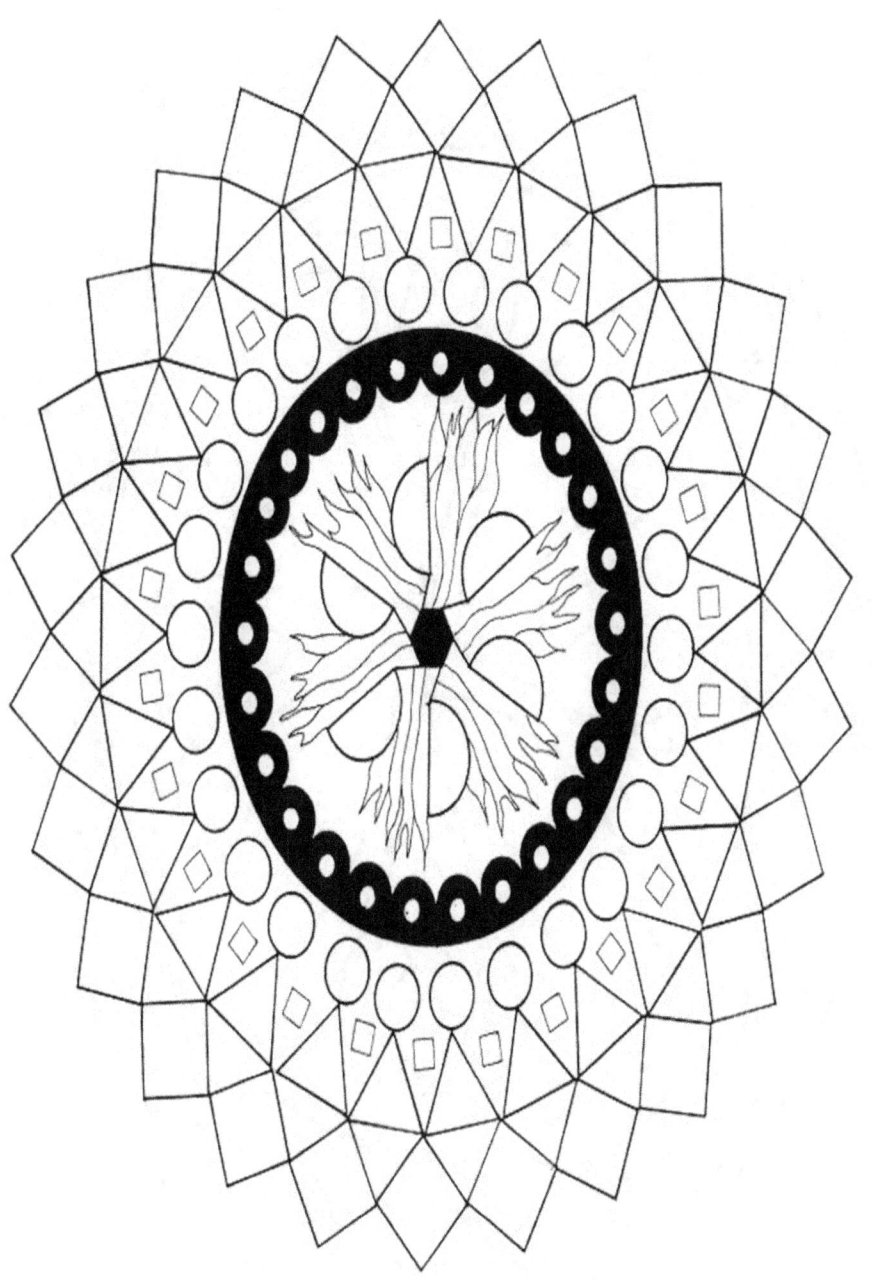

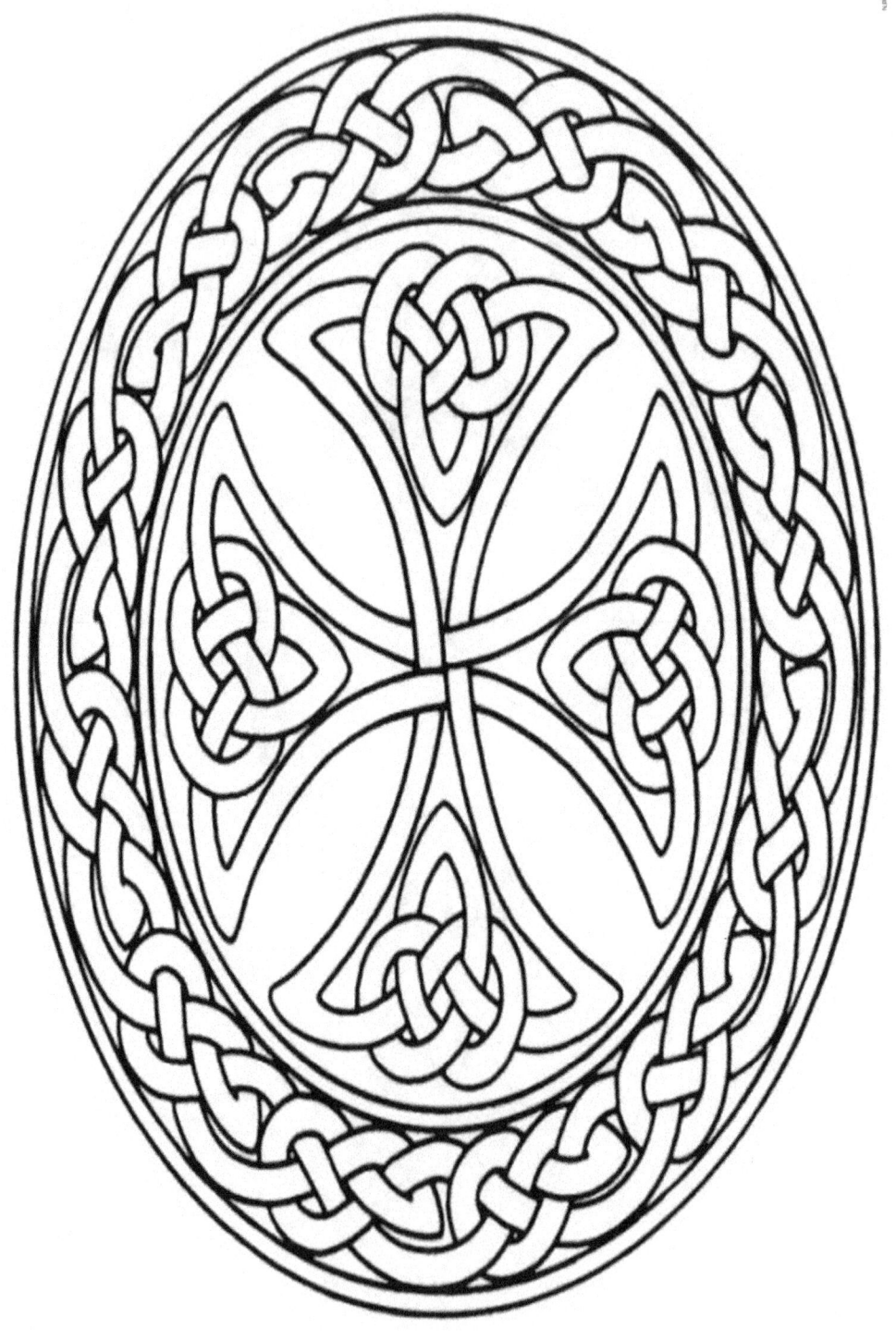

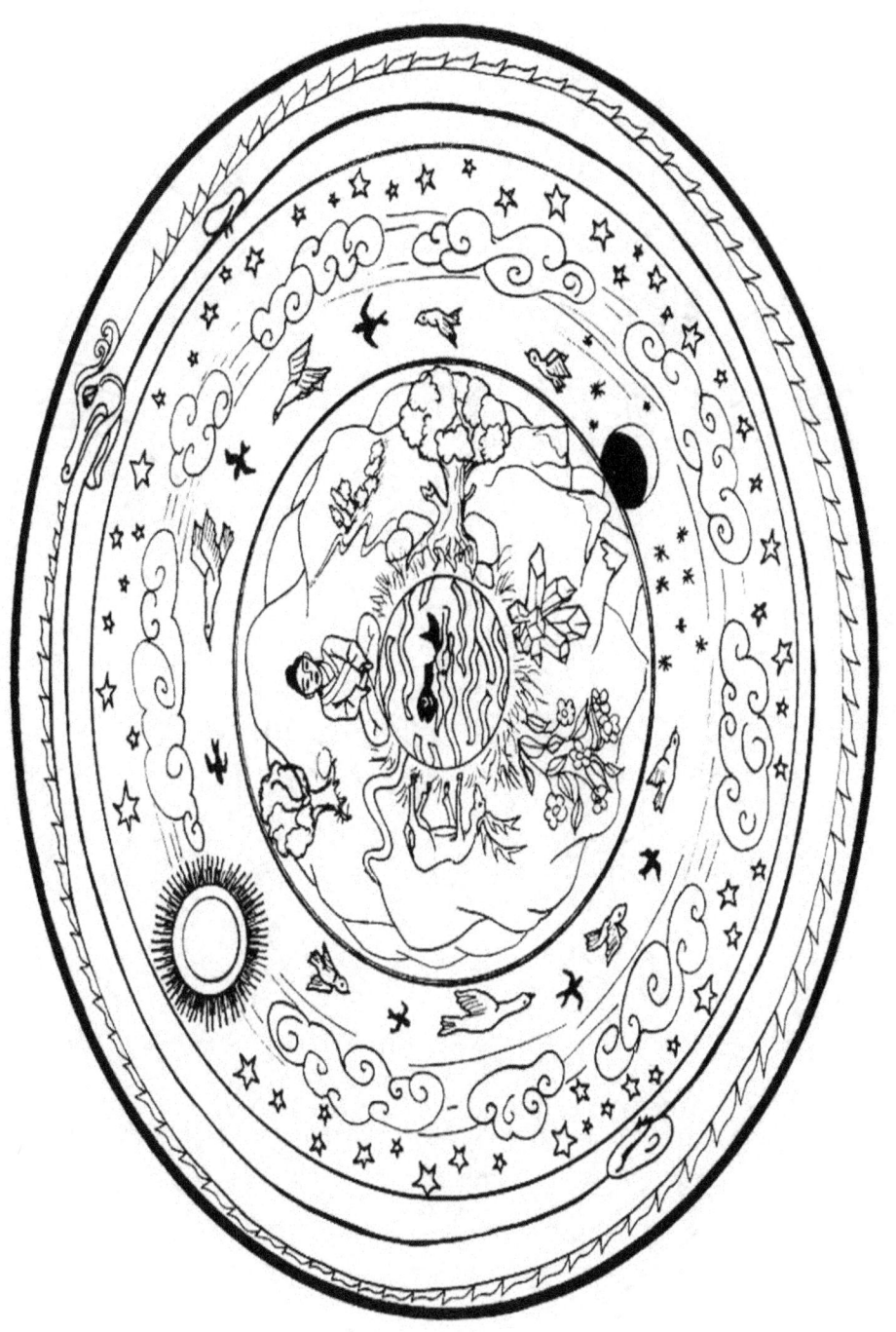

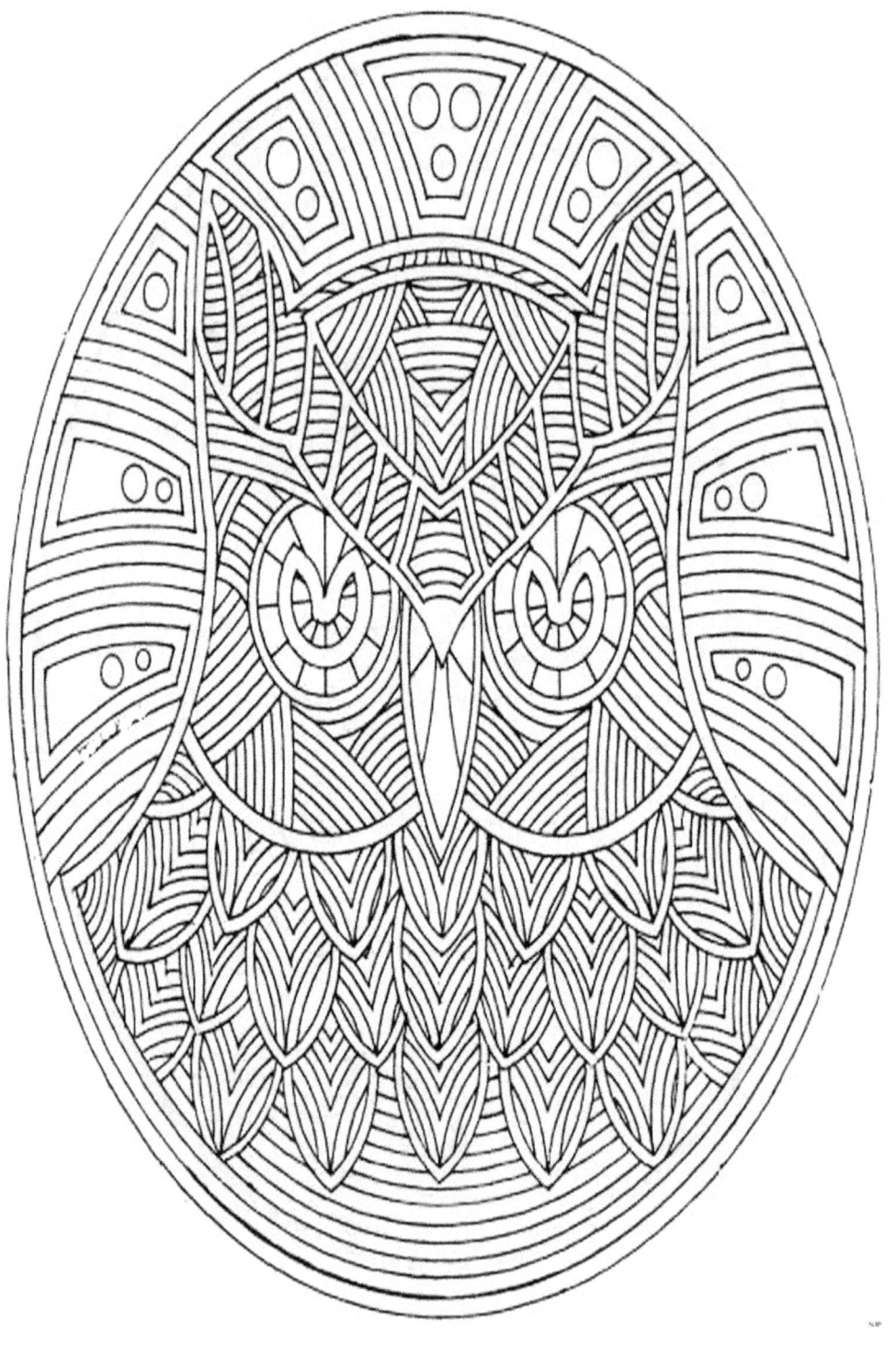

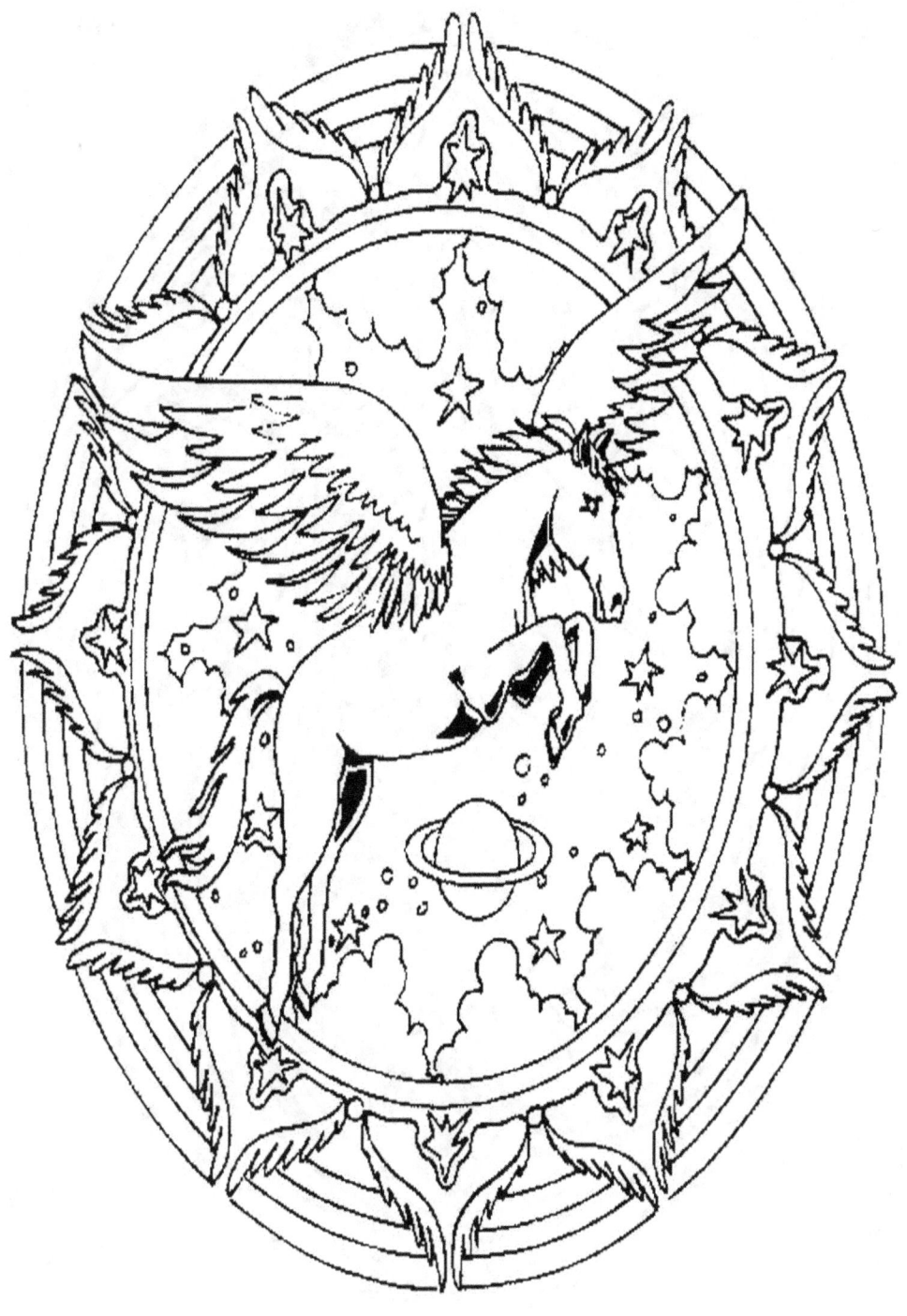

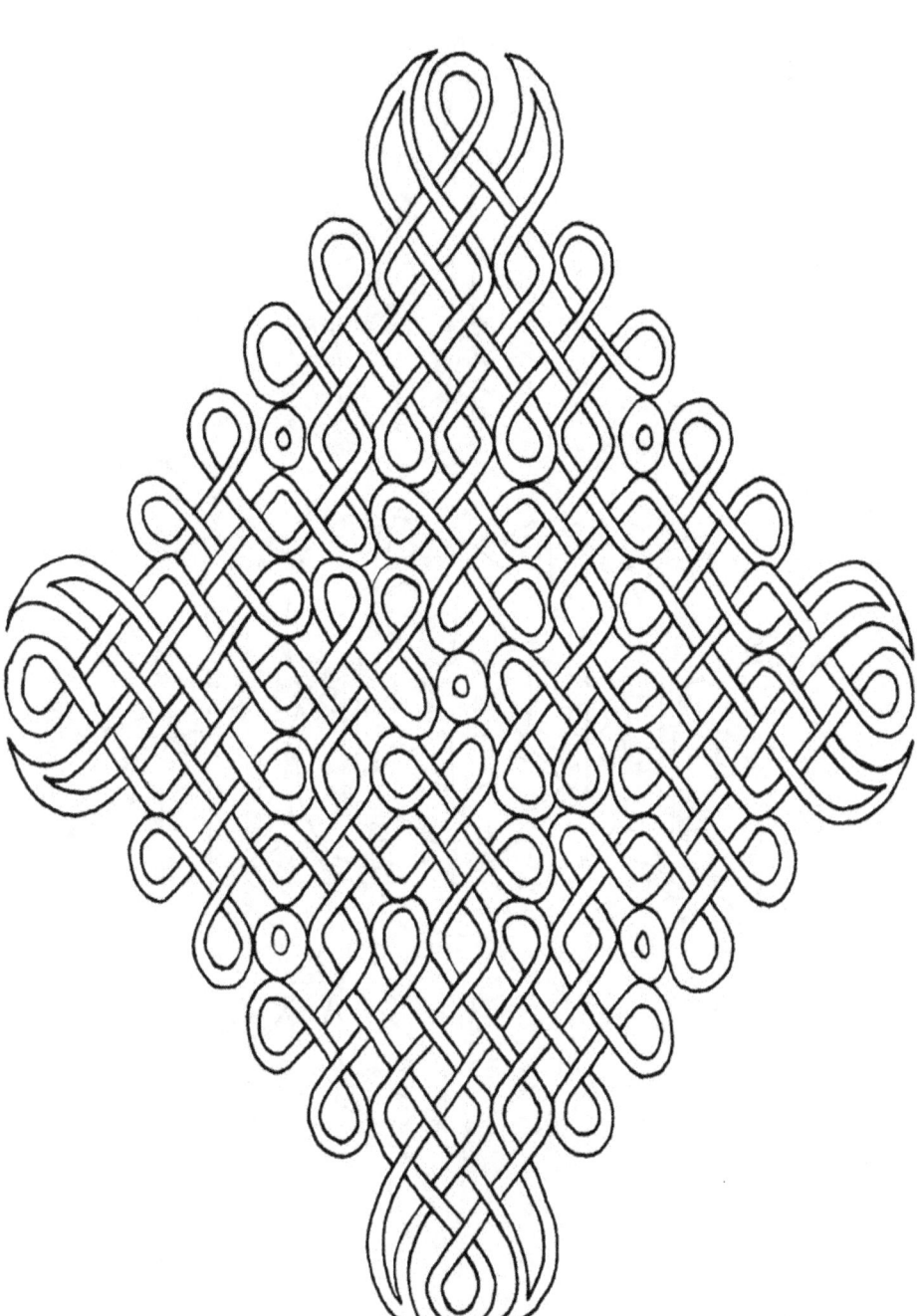

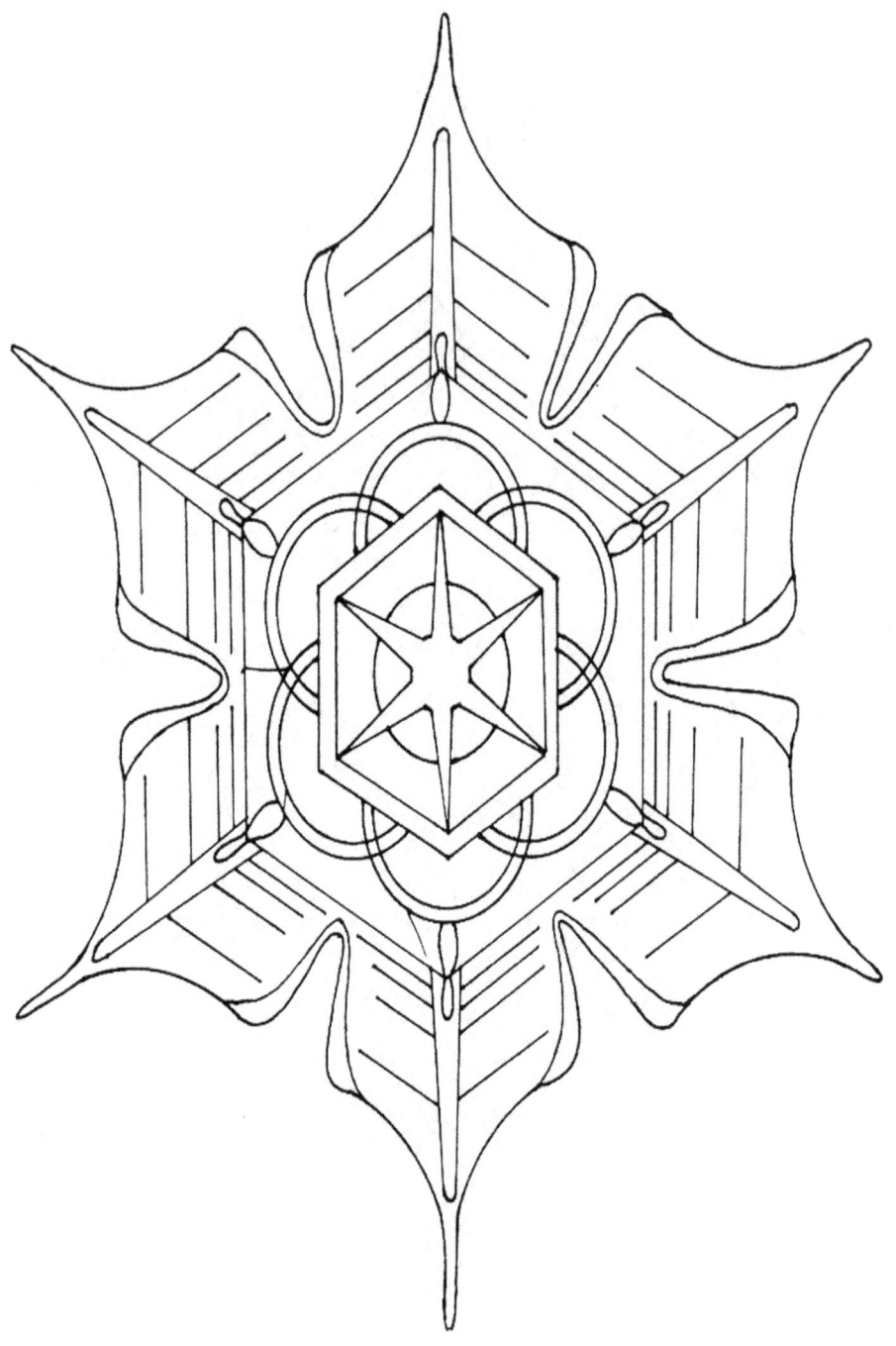

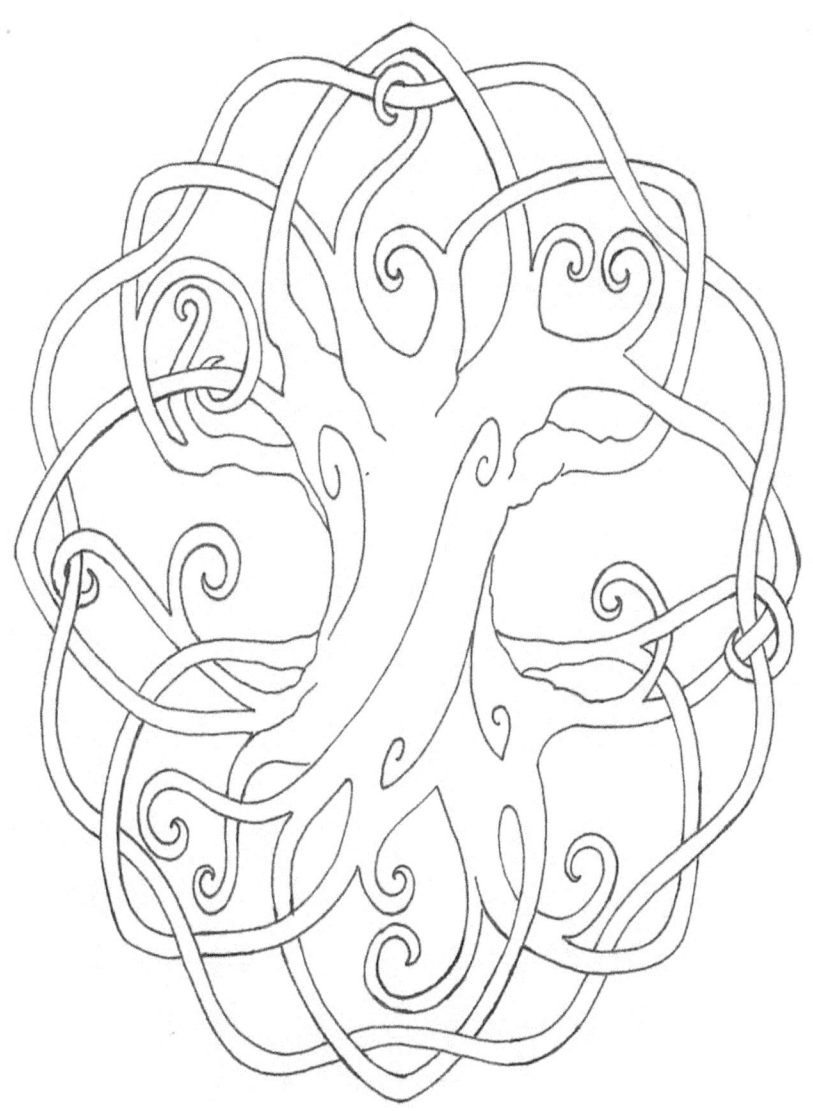

www.ingramcontent.com/pod-product-compliance
Lightning Source LLC
Chambersburg PA
CBHW080614190526
45169CB00007B/3010